The Debt Problem for Poor Countries

Where Are We?

A Report on Illegitimate Debt and Arbitration

edited by

Rogate R. Mshana

This document is the report of the Illegitimate Debt and Arbitration Workshop held in Geneva from 30th June to 2nd July 2003.

It will also serve as a background paper for furthering the debate on global debt cancellation.

150, route de Ferney, P.O. Box 2100
1211 Geneva 2, Switzerland
Web site: http://www.wcc-coe.org
ISBN 2-8254-1409-3

Contents

Foreword

The issue of poor countries in debt is not yet resolved, despite the huge global campaign waged for almost a decade by civil society. At most, civil society has succeeded in raising awareness that such debt is the result of an unjust financial system, which has to be addressed from a justice perspective. The response from rich countries was the announcement of the Heavily Indebted Poor Countries initiative (HIPC) at Köln in 1998. Debt cancellation campaigners - using a variety of methods - continued to put pressure on rich countries to 'Drop the Debt' by 2000, as part of a Jubilee for a debt-free millennium. This never happened. In the meantime, the HIPC and its operational mechanisms have proved inadequate to address the root causes of debt. Rich countries have not seriously addressed the problem, as witnessed in many of their self-appointed gatherings, such as the G7 summits. The civil societies to which churches belong have realized that new strategies and strong alliances for continued pressure are imperative.

While civil society continues to campaign, various creative, contradictory and complementary tactics have emerged. Some have focused on the technical aspects of the debt problem. Others have concentrated on legal aspects (e.g. arbitration mechanisms, an arbitration court, insolvency law). Other tactics are more political (e.g. repudiation, tribunals and plebiscites), while others are mathematical in nature, focusing on levels of relief from debt and the role of debt relief in promoting development (e.g. proposals for new debt sustainability levels by changing thresholds). Even more significantly, while some speak of debt relief, others speak of total debt cancellation: 'Don't Owe, Won't Pay.' Such divisions in views and methods were visible in 1998 in Köln among the Jubilee 2000 campaigners. The rift between Jubilee 2000 and Jubilee South became evident after the latter's formation and consolidation in Johannesburg in 1998.

In observing activities at the World Social Forum and various panels of non-governmental organizations at the meetings of the United Nations and international financial institutions, it was clear that such contradictory approaches sent conflicting messages to IFIs, the G7 and the UN. The World Council of Churches took up the challenge of reconciling the different groups. Consultations were held in Africa, Europe and North America in 2000 and 2001. In 2002 it was hoped that a united front would emerge, but this did not happen. Thus, it remains necessary for us to re-examine our strategies, commonalties and differences in order to form the basis for a powerful campaign. This requires cooperation and genuine sharing. No one single group can bring about change by itself.

The World Council of Churches organized a workshop on illegitimate debt and arbitration, held in Geneva from 30 June to 2 July, 2003. The main aims of the workshop were to assess the ongoing campaign in light of current geopolitics and how to resolve the issue of debt as efficiently and fairly as possible. About thirty participants were drawn from debt campaign organizations and movements from Africa, Asia, the Pacific, Latin America, Europe and North America.

This book describes the initiatives of debt cancellation movements around the world. So far, their various proposals for solving the problem of debt have not penetrated centres of power such as the G8, the World Bank and the International Monetary Fund. The IMF's own proposal for a Sovereign Debt Restructuring Mechanism has been unanimously rejected by all the movements for debt cancellation.

What next? This is the question that challenges us all.

Rogate R. Mshana
Programme Executive, Economic Justice
World Council of Churches

March 2004

1

Fair and Transparent Arbitration On Debt

African Forum and Network on Debt and Development

INTRODUCTION

This chapter is an attempt to help move the debate on debt in Africa beyond the unfulfilled demands for debt cancellation made by severely indebted low-income countries and global civil society.

Total cancellation of both bilateral and multilateral debt would provide finance for economic and human development. For Africa, this could mean a minimum of US$13 billion per year. However, legitimate demands for debt cancellation have not met with a genuine and positive response from creditor governments and institutions. As donors, creditor governments and institutions continue to dominate decisions about debt relief initiatives. Such decisions tend to prioritize the maintenance and protection of the international financial system and exhibit little real concern for the development of people in indebted countries.

Only fair and transparent global governance will protect the interests of weak debtor nations and their people. A structural change is required to help reshape global relations around the debt crisis. Global civil society, African governments and intergovernmental institutions should work for the establishment of a fair and transparent arbitration mechanism under the auspices of the United Nations, as part of a sustainable solution to the debt crisis. Various options are available at the global level to deal with the problem. We suggest that an international arbitration court is both feasible and long overdue.

The persistence of the debt crisis and the inability of the international community to find immediate and sustainable solutions has raised legitimate concern and brought to the fore the need for global structural change. There are many facets to the debt crisis, but the fundamental problem is that the creditors - who constitute the donors - continue to dominate decision-making. For many years, debt relief initiatives have been designed by donors to safeguard their interests. A democratic or rights-based framework for resolution of the debt crisis is therefore necessary.

It is important to note from the outset that the debt problem is inextricably tied to other factors (political, economic and social) in both creditor and debtor countries. These factors - not the absence of a dispute settlement system - are mainly responsible for the current level of southern debt. Another main contributory factor to the persistence and magnitude of the debt crisis is the intransigence of some northern creditors (states, international financial institutions (IFIs) and commercial banks) in the face of calls for debt cancellation or reduction. The need for a fair and transparent arbitration mechanism is itself based on the necessity for resolving the power imbalance between creditors and debtors.

BACKGROUND AND RATIONALE FOR ARBITRATION

Arbitration is one of the alternative methods for resolving a dispute outside the traditional court system. In this process, a third independent party provides a final decision on a dispute.

A 'dispute' in the arbitration process can be defined to include the existence of divergent or opposing views which cannot be reconciled by two parties, and which therefore requires a third party to decide which view should prevail, depending on the arguments presented by the two parties. Arbitration agreements allow for settlement or final decisions to be made on grounds other than purely legal principles, such as considerations of justice, equity and human rights. In the case of the debt problem, divergent or opposing views between debtors and the creditors could be subject to arbitration.

There is an absolute need for cancellation of official bilateral and multilateral debts. While debtors have made undisputed and legitimate claims for such debt cancellation, creditors claim it is not needed. Thus, debt cancellation can be a subject of arbitration.

Calls for debt cancellation have been made in the following contexts (to name a few):

- Jubilee 2000 movement, which collected millions of signatures from all over the world calling for total debt cancellation. It was ignored by creditor governments and IFIs.
- The Secretary General's Report (December 2000) to the Financing for Development Preparatory Committee meetings noted the difficult debt situation confronted by heavily indebted low-income countries (no matter how skilled their economic management) and that there are cases where debt cancellation could be called for.
- The Third United Nations Conference on the Least Developed Countries (UN LDC-III), which was held in Brussels in May 2001, fully acknowledged that the external debt of the majority of LDCs constitutes an obstacle to their development and growth; that debt servicing comprises a large part of scarce budgetary resources that could be directed to productive and social areas; and that debt overhang affects the internal and external investment climate. Creditors, however, were unwilling to undertake debt cancellation: they opted for providing Official Development Assistance, with a view to ensuring that these countries do not fall back into arrears. Clearly, this type of debt relief is directed at safeguarding loan repayments to creditors rather than working towards the interests of the people in debtor countries.
- The African ministers of finance meeting in Addis Ababa in November 2000 - as part of the Regional Meetings on Financing for Development - called for an independent body (i.e. one that would not be unduly influenced by the interests of creditors) to examine the Heavily Indebted Poor Countries initiative (HIPC) and other debt stressed countries in respect to debt reduction, conditionalities and other issues. The meeting also called-for a debt servicing moratorium (including accrued interest) in order to allow African countries to find lasting solutions to their debt problems.

- The High Level Panel appointed by the UN secretary general to provide expert opinion on various issues in the context of the Financing for Development process, led by Ernesto Zedillo, recognized the existence of the debt crisis and the inadequacies of the current debt relief initiative, to the extent of anticipating an HIPC-III.

The assumption of current debt relief initiatives is that debtor countries are solely responsible for the crisis. While accepting part of the responsibility (due to lack of proper debt management, corruption and other shortcomings), debtors point to the impact of external factors, including the existence of a global trade regime in which debtor countries continue to suffer declines in terms of trade and ongoing lack of global market access; natural disasters; inappropriate policy advice from the International Monetary Fund (IMF) and World Bank; and push factors in lending.

Creditors are seldom viewed as part of the problem, which they obviously are. Creditor-initiated and imposed debt relief initiatives, such as HIPC, do not address the crisis adequately. They are meant to protect the interests of creditors and the international financial system, rather than those of debtor countries and their people.

Arbitration is needed on specific types of loans or debt, in particular odious and illegitimate debts such as the following:

- Debts that cannot be serviced without causing harm to people and communities. It is a violation of human rights to repay debt at the expense of meeting human developmental needs.
- Debts incurred by illegitimate debtors and creditors acting illegitimately, including odious debts and stolen loans.
- Debts incurred from illegitimate uses, such as projects that did not benefit people.
- Debt incurred through wrong policy advice or as a result of external factors over which debtors have no control.

One of the major reasons for the lack of political will to resolve the debt crisis is that creditors see the protection of the international financial system as the basis for decisions. Debtors, on the other hand, argue that a human rights criterion would better reflect the so-called partnership that is expected to exist between developed and developing countries. The criteria for making decisions about debt cancellation lend themselves to arbitration.

Appropriate instruments and institutions are required to deal with the debt problem. Existing instruments, such as the Permanent Court of Arbitration based in the Hague, and the United Nations Commission on Trade, could have their mandates extended to include debt issues, or a new commission specifically for debt could be established. We believe the best solution is to set up an international arbitration court on debt through a treaty.

LEGAL ISSUES

Arbitration in general

Arbitration is the procedure whereby parties to a dispute refer that dispute to a third party for a final decision. It has been a means of dispute resolution for many thousands of years in various cultures in the world. It is a means of 'alternative' dispute resolution, as it is an alternative to other, especially legal, means of dispute resolution. Speaking in the context of trade and investment disputes, Nelson Mandela said:

> We have a special interest in alternative dispute resolution. It is an approach that has stood us in good stead through our negotiated transition and has taken root in the field of labour and community conflict. (Message to the Conference on the Resolution of International Trade and Investment Disputes in Africa, March 1997)

Arbitration agreements may allow for a settlement to be made on grounds other than purely legal principles, such as considerations of justice, equity and human rights.

What constitutes a dispute should be widely interpreted. The International Court of Justice has stated: 'A dispute is a disagreement on a point of law or fact, a conflict of legal views or of interests between two persons.' However broad the understanding of what constitutes a dispute might be, it is clear that in principle a simple failure to pay a debt does not constitute a dispute, although this may naturally lead to a 'conflict of interests' between the parties. The International Court of Justice in the Southwest Africa case stated:

> A mere ascertation is not sufficient to prove the existence of a dispute ... Nor is it adequate to show that the interests of the two parties are in conflict. It must be shown that the claim of one party is positively opposed by the other.

Other forms of resolving conflict

Negotiation

Disputes such as those that might arise around debt are inevitable in international relations. Negotiations between states are usually conducted through normal diplomatic channels or through competent government ministries. Any disagreements render issues to be taken to the highest level of government.

Mediation

When the parties to an international or domestic dispute are unable to resolve matters by negotiation, the intervention of a third party is a possible means of breaking the impasse and producing an acceptable solution. The third party may simply encourage the disputants to resume negotiations, or do nothing more than provide them with an additional channel of communication. A mediator may actively participate in discussions and advance their own proposals, or interpret and transmit each party's proposals to the other.

Mediation may be performed by organizations, states, or individuals and cannot be forced on the parties to an international dispute without prior consent having been obtained.

Conciliation
Conciliation has been defined as:

> A method for the settlement of international disputes of any nature according to which a Commission set up by the Parties, either on a permanent basis or an ad hoc basis to deal with a dispute, proceeds to the impartial examination of the dispute and attempts to define the terms of a settlement susceptible of being accepted by them or of affording the Parties, with a view to its settlement, such aid as they may have requested. (Article 1 of the Regulations on the Procedure of International Conciliation adopted by the Institute of International Law, 1961)

If mediation is essentially an extension of negotiation, conciliation puts third-party intervention on a formal legal footing and institutionalizes it in a way comparable to, but not identical with, inquiry or arbitration. Fact finding - the essence of inquiry - may or may not be an important element in conciliation, while the search for non-binding terms susceptible of acceptance by the parties provides a sharp contrast with arbitration and a reminder of the link between conciliation and mediation. All conciliation commissions have the same functions: to investigate a dispute and suggest the terms of a possible settlement.

Advantages and disadvantages of arbitration
The main advantages of arbitration include choice of arbiters by the parties, choice of procedure (potentially non-adversarial), the neutrality of the arbitrator and the enforceability of award at international law. Arbitration of commercial disputes can often be difficult, lengthy and costly. Most difficulties arise when parties fail to agree on preliminary matters, such as rules or procedures, venue(s) and the language of hearings. One would expect for debt issues there would be fewer such problems. However, a treaty may be necessary to establish the ground for parties to submit to arbitration.

Arbitration in international law
Arbitration has a long history in international law and is a well-established means of resolving disputes between states and nationals of different states. Arbitration can be seen as a move away from the power-based system of negotiated settlements towards a more principled system.

International conventions on arbitration
The majority of international conventions on arbitration deal with the international recognition of agreements to arbitrate and the recognition and enforcement of foreign arbitral awards. The 1923 Geneva Protocol and the 1927 Geneva Convention laid the foundation for the widely accepted 1958 New York

Convention on the Recognition and Enforcement of Foreign Arbitral Awards (the New York Convention).

In the New York Convention, contracting states agree to recognize and enforce arbitral awards made in other contracting states. Some states agree to do so only on the basis of reciprocity. The Convention further details the grounds on which recognition and enforcement of foreign awards can be refused. On the whole, the Convention provides a legal framework that would uphold arbitrations on debt. Some 126 states have acceded to the New York Convention.

Existing arbitral institutions

Current arbitrations are largely commercial in nature, involving trade, commerce, private sector loan agreements and investments. Aside from the various arbitration institutions at the national level, there is the International Centre for the Settlement of Investment Disputes (ICSID), the International Chamber of Commerce International Court of Arbitration, and the United Nations Commission on International Trade Law (UNCITRAL).

Loan agreements involving state parties are usually perceived as transactions of a commercial nature, although particular difficulties arising from the sovereign immunity of states and the existing economic and political environment would appear to have prevented a more widespread use of the commercial arbitral mechanism to resolve debt problems. The most relevant instrument for handling arbitrations on debt problems as not being purely commercial in nature is the Permanent Court of Arbitration (PCA)

The mandate of UNCITRAL and ICSID could be expanded to cover debt. However, ICSID would have to be independent of the World Bank, since the bank is a lender and will most likely be a party to arbitration on multilateral debt.

The Permanent Court of Arbitration

The PCA, residing in the Hague, was created by the 1899 and 1907 Hague Peace Conference. It acts as a registry for arbitral tribunals created ad hoc for specific disputes and maintains a panel of persons, nominated by contracting states, from which states may choose arbitrators to adjudicate their disputes. States must accede to the PCA conventions to access its facilities. In 1962 the PCA began to accept disputes between states and 'non-state' organizations or individuals. In 1996 it adopted a set of Optional Rules based on the UNCITRAL Arbitration Rules. The PCA thus has rules in relation to arbitrating disputes between states (for bilateral debt issues), between states and international organizations (for multilateral debt; e.g., World Bank and IMF), and between two parties of which only one is a state (for private debt, public guaranteed debts and stolen money). The rules governing arbitration between two parties of which only one is a state would allow for civil society to take up a case for arbitration at the PCA.

An appropriate framework for the resolution of debt is an organization established by treaty, convention or UN General Assembly resolution. The treaty or convention establishing the organization should deal with issues of sovereignty and the waiver of sovereignty and perhaps with the locus standi of parties and groups of affected persons to approach the tribunal.

The organization should also operate within well-defined rules, possess a small secretariat to assist in the administration of arbitrations, and act as a decisive authority where parties cannot agree (on issues such as venue, appointment of arbitrators, etc.). The PCA is a good example of an organization with all of these characteristics.

The UNCITRAL Model Law

UNCITRAL drafted its Model Law on International Commercial Arbitration, completed in 1985. The aim of the Model Law was to harmonize national legislation on arbitration. Features include the protection of party autonomy, the upholding of the principles of natural justice in the conduct of hearings, and the limited circumstances in which national courts may interfere in the arbitral process. Legislation based on the Model Law has been enacted in at least 37 countries.

UNCITRAL additionally provides training and technical assistance to states, including (a) information activities aimed at promoting understanding of international commercial law conventions, model laws, and other legal texts; (b) assistance to member states with commercial law reform and adoption of UNCITRAL texts; and (c) assistance to chambers of commerce and professional associations with the use of UNCITRAL non-legislative texts as models for preparing their own rules or with the direct use of those texts by their members. As in the case of the PCA, UNICTRAL could prove to be a good framework for arbitration on debt if its mandate were expanded to include debt. Alternatively, the UN could establish a Commission on debt based on the same model as UNICTRAL. (The UNCITRAL Notes on Organizing Arbitral Proceedings provide a useful guide to arranging arbitrations. The UNCITRAL rules, as well as the rules of existing institutions such as the PCA's Optional Rules, are also useful reference materials.)

The International Centre for the Settlement of Investment Disputes

ICSID was established by the 1966 Washington Convention on the Settlement of Investment Disputes between States and Nationals of Other States, in order to provide a dispute resolution mechanism separate from the national laws of states for disputes between states and non-state entities. The ICSID Convention is widely used and has been ratified by 120 state parties.

Extending debt arbitration to this centre would again have to be conditional on its independence from the World Bank (the bank is a lender and also very close to other lenders), otherwise its neutrality would be compromised and debtors would be reluctant to submit to the arbitrations it administered or organized.

While, for example, the neutrality of ICSID may be in doubt, parties to disputes have the comfort of some degree of neutrality of process, as in most cases they may select their own arbitrator or arbitrators. ICSID provides that where parties cannot agree on an arbitrator, each side should propose an arbitrator, both of whom then agree on a third.

Arbitration centres

Many 'arbitration centres' have been established around the world (including African countries), which concentrate on promoting the resolution of commercial disputes. Typically, these centres are not-for-profit organizations that facilitate the training of arbitrators and maintain a database of arbitrators for suggestion to parties to disputes. They may additionally provide services in support of arbitrations underway: arranging venues, the recording and transcription of hearings, translators and other general administrative and secretarial tasks.

These arbitration centres represent a local skill base consisting of a nucleus of trained and experienced arbitrators. Not only can arbitration centres be a source of arbitral experts, but also they can provide a skills base in the hosting and facilitation of the arbitral process. Where appropriate, this opens up the possibility of the successful use of many debtor states as venues for the conduct of an international arbitration.

On agreement between the parties, an arbitration can be hosted in any suitable place. Some arbitration hearings are held in several locations, for example with parties holding agreed preliminary meetings in the territory of one party and the final hearing in the territory of another. Where parties are physically located in different jurisdictions this may have the effect of splitting the cost and inconvenience of travel and accommodation in a foreign territory. Debtor states should be encouraged to investigate such options and where appropriate negotiate to achieve them.

The use of existing institutions by 'developing' states

> It takes time, and it costs money, to conduct a major international commercial arbitration, whether or not one of the parties is a state. Hearing and conference rooms have to be hired; and often it will prove necessary to appoint a secretary or registrar to assist the tribunal in its work, together with translators, stenographers and so on. At the PCA, rooms for hearings and the services of the Bureau are provided to parties for a nominal charge. This is an obvious attraction. It is surprising that more use is not made of these facilities ... The only requirement for recourse to the expertise of the Bureau, and the excellent and prestigious facilities of the Peace Palace, is that the state concerned should be, or become, a party to either the Hague Convention of 1899 or that of 1907. (Redfurn and Hunter, Law and Practice of International Commercial Arbitration, 2nd edn: 46)

UN Secretary General Kofi Annan, in a foreword to a collection of PCA documents, states:

> I encourage states, international organizations and private parties to make greater use of the Court's services, which also include fact finding and conciliation; such recourse would help ease the workload of the International Court of Justice and fill gaps concerning arbitrations involving private parties and international organizations. I also urge states which have not ratified the Hague Conventions to do so. Developing countries, in particular, could well find the flexible instruments of dispute resolution to be an invaluable asset.

Before an informed decision can be made on whether or not to use the PCA or another framework, detailed information is required about anticipated disputes and consultations should be undertaken with relevant governments and the PCA.

Many third world countries have been deeply distrustful of arbitration for the settlement of international disputes ... bias against developing countries was perceived in the attitude and awards of international arbitrators. (I. Okekeifere, 'Enhancing the implementation of economic projects in the third world through arbitration', Journal of the Chartered Institute of Arbitrators. August 2001: 240, 242)

In more recent times, however, there has been a trend towards the use of arbitration, as arbitration laws and infrastructures are established in developing countries and a local skills base has developed. As Okekeifere states, more recently 'there has been a steady progress towards a warm embrace of international and domestic arbitration ... most of the third world states have established a sophisticated legal infrastructure for the governance and conduct of arbitration.'

Despite this trend, many developing states tend not to use 'home grown' arbitrators and legal representatives to resolve their disputes. Since the PCA allows for parties to choose the arbitrators, debtor countries will need to be encouraged to use their domestic skills at the PCA.

Sovereign Immunity and Arbitration

In international law, sovereign states possess a degree of immunity from private tribunals or the courts of other states. Submission to an arbitral tribunal would require the waiver of sovereign immunity with respect to the matter at hand by sovereign states, failing which the tribunal would not have the authority to determine the dispute.

Whether sovereign immunity is total or partial is a matter of some debate. Some authors promote the doctrine of Restrictive Immunity: states, when conducting affairs of a private law nature or jure gestitonis, should be treated as the natural subjects of private law. However, as Brownlie notes:

> It is far from easy to state the current legal position in terms of customary or general international law. Recent writers emphasize that there is a trend in the practice of states towards the restrictive doctrine of immunity but avoid firm and precise prescriptions as to the present state of the law.

What is clear is that 'voluntary submission to jurisdiction does not extend to measures of execution.' Waivers of immunity could be on a case-by-case basis or by means of a blanket waiver in respect of disputes resulting from foreign debt. For the avoidance of doubt, it is advisable that the waiver in either case be explicit: some national courts will not imply a waiver from general circumstances and it is possible, although unlikely, that an arbitral tribunal might take the same approach.

States should carefully weigh the consequences and those desirous of maintaining as much immunity as possible should be careful to word restrictively any such waiver. A blanket waiver could be achieved in a treaty or declaration, but should likewise be carefully worded and considered. Due to the broad nature of disputes possible in debt situations, a blanket waiver might be considered advisable.

Locus standi of 'Debt Affected Peoples'

Civil society organizations (CSOs) are eager to see peoples affected by debt to have the basic right, locus standi, to bring cases before an arbitration tribunal. The effects of a loan may be relevant when assessing its worth, and hardship caused by a debt may lend moral force to the argument to cancel or forgive the debt, but it does not create a legal relationship between lenders and citizens of debtor states, except possibly as these citizens are represented by their governments in agreements with lenders. Thus, conventional wisdom has it that while affected peoples may have a genuine grievance resulting from debt-induced hardships, this does not in itself result in a justifiable dispute between those affected and the lender.

Furthermore, debtor states themselves may wish to guard their right (and the privileges that go with this right) to represent their citizens at international level. It is not inconceivable that a grouping of affected people may make a submission or take a case to a tribunal in conflict with the wishes of the debtor state of which they are citizens. If a grouping of affected people is sufficiently small and unrepresentative of general feeling within the debtor state, or if the cost of appearing before a tribunal means only those with significant funds are able to do so, minority views and concerns might conceivably be given disproportionate weight. Consultations may need to be conducted with debtor governments to ascertain what their view on this issue is likely to be.

It is also considered most unlikely that any lending institution would voluntarily submit to a process whereby persons, groups of persons or organizations that are not a party to the lender's agreement with the borrower could challenge the validity of the relevant agreement. Accordingly, the achievement of the right of locus standi for affected peoples to appear in debt arbitrations, except as they already have through their democratically elected governments, may prove to be difficult in current circumstances.

The other side of the coin to this argument, however, is that although civil society is not party to loan agreements, it is nevertheless a key stakeholder, as it is directly affected by the decisions and consequences of such loan agreements. On the basis of equity, human rights and justice, as well as the human rights enshrined in the UN Charter and the Arusha Charter on Popular Participation (the African Charter, 1990, which promotes people-centred development), the people affected by debt problems have the fundamental right to be heard and may therefore bring cases for arbitration. In this respect they have the right to do so under the PCA rules governing arbitration between two parties of which only one is a state.

Validity of Debts

The jurisdiction of an arbitral tribunal need not be limited to deciding on strictly legal principles, but may also consider principles of human rights, justice and equity.

It is conceivable that disputes over validity could arise from questions concerning the gross negligence of a lender or false representations made by a lender or its agents, and issues such as disagreements over the calculation of interest and repayments, etc. Typically, loan agreements often contain clauses that exclude liability for the lender and its agents. As a matter of policy, governments should not accept the broad exclusion of liability clauses, which unfairly benefits lenders.

In many jurisdictions, however, exclusion of one's own liability is not permitted in cases of extreme or gross negligence. Research should be undertaken to determine what portion of Africa's debt is governed by such laws and is challengeable on the grounds of gross negligence of the lender.

It is useful to quote from the UNITAR Resource Centre Training Package:

> Developing countries rely on external expertise because they lack the technical know-how and assistance to plan infrastructure policies and to implement projects. Consequently, developing countries should not bear the burden of that bad planning and bad implementation performed by external sources. Consultants should not be paid and must be held liable for insufficient studies, which lead to wasteful projects and cause prejudice to the country. Contractors who fail to perform should also be held liable; financial institutions are not exempt from liabilities. Sectoral comparative law studies indicate that modern civil and commercial law has broadened contractual obligations in complex business transactions beyond the strict delivery of goods, performance of services, or payment of money to include dissemination of professional information, exchange of motivated opinions, discovery of special risks, and instructions and consultations, especially if one party is less knowledgeable than the other and therefore must trust the other's superior skills. Neglecting these accessory obligations may be considered a breach of contract, which entitles the other party to damages and discharges it from obligations. These tendencies exist in purely commercial transactions and should be all the more applicable if the lender is an official donor with the statutory obligation to finance and assist in the execution of development projects.

Illegitimate and odious debts

Illegitimacy of debt is based on the following principles:

- Debts contracted by dictatorships or repressive regimes and used to strengthen the hold of those regimes are illegitimate; for instance, the apartheid-caused debt inherited by South Africa (an established legal principle, as discussed above).
- A debt contracted by corrupt governments and stolen by leaders and senior public officials is illegitimate. This has also been referred to as stolen wealth (for instance, the late President Mobutu of Zaire).
- Debts contracted and used for improperly designed projects and programmes are illegitimate. There is a heavy responsibility on creditors here, particularly on the World Bank for its failed development projects (so-called white elephant projects, etc.) and the IMF for the failure of its prescriptions.

- Debts that swelled because of high interest rates and other conditions imposed by creditor governments and banks are illegitimate. This view argues that the original debt (the principle) has already been paid many times over, so the continued existence of a debt burden is illegitimate.
- Debts which cannot be serviced without impoverishing a country's people are illegitimate. This is more often termed immoral debt. As the late Julius Nyerere said, 'Must we starve our children to pay our debts?'
- All debts owed by the South to the North can be considered illegitimate. As Jubilee South maintains, the countries of the South are in fact the creditors for a historical, social and ecological debt which northern countries refuse to recognize.

Stolen wealth

Nothing precludes the submission of a dispute to arbitration involving the return of money stolen or obtained through corruption by officials or former officials of a state to that state. Should an appropriate arbitration framework for the resolution of debt be identified or established, it may be that this framework will also be well suited to the resolution of such 'stolen money' disputes.

An investigation or survey to assess the laws governing debt and the statutory and other obligations of lenders and to determine the consequent portion of illegitimate debt by a neutral organization may be appropriate. In this respect the UN, an agency of the UN, or even an intergovernmental body like the African Union, might play a useful role. It will be important for any neutral investigative body - and particularly important for the UN - to be seen to be investigating fairly without preconceptions or prejudice. It is likely that not all states will be comfortable with UN involvement and it may be necessary for debtor states wishing for a detailed survey to commission their own and submit their debts to a survey conducted by a private organization or their own legal experts. One advantage of such a survey is that debtor states would be better informed about loan agreements that might be successfully challenged. Should debtor states show a willingness to proceed to challenge loan agreements using arbitration, at the very least this would give them a stronger position from which to negotiate in their drive for debt reduction and cancellation.

Implications of Arbitrating on Debt

Success or failure before an arbitral tribunal will naturally depend on a variety of factors. The strength or weakness of the case presented and the basis on which it is decided are of obvious importance to an assessment of the likely outcome.

Arbitrations do not usually use a precedent system. Should there be no precedent system, it is not anticipated that a failure in any one case would necessarily prejudice the success of any further cases on the same grounds.

Establishment of an international arbitration court

The unique problems of debt call for the establishment of a special court. Many arbitral institutions in the world do not restrict their settlement disputes to one mode. Rather, they employ methods and processes appropriate for each particular dispute. It would not be appropriate to enhance current mechanisms (such as the Paris Club) by introducing arbitration panels to hear possible disputes between debtors and creditors, because such a club (which is in fact a cartel) can still intimidate debtors under the guise of debt negotiation. The imbalances in bargaining power between creditors and debtors call for the establishment of a neutral and impartial arbitral institution.

The establishment of a unique arbitral institution to deal with the problem of debt is further justified by the fact that similar institutions have been set up before to deal with unique problems. As noted above, these include ICSID and the PCA.

It is desirable that the proposed court be set up under the UN and by international treaty. According to Article 3 of the United Nations Charter, members have agreed to 'settle their international disputes by peaceful means in such a manner that international peace and security, and justice, are not endangered'. A General Assembly Resolution of 1970 quotes Article 2 (3) of the UN Charter and proclaims:

> States shall accordingly seek early and just settlement of their international disputes by negotiation, inquiry, mediation, conciliation, arbitration, judicial settlement, resort to regional agencies or arrangements or other peaceful means of their choice.

Establishing the proposed court under the auspices of the United Nations would therefore be the most logical step. In this regard, many conventions relating to arbitration have been enacted under the auspices of the UN. Some examples are the Protocol on Arbitration Clauses of 1923, the Convention on the Execution of Foreign Arbitral Award of 1927, the Convention on the Recognition and Enforcement of Foreign Arbitral Awards (New York), 1958, the United Nations Commission on International Trade Law (UNCITRAL) Arbitration Rules, UNCITRAL Conciliation Rules, UNCITRAL Model Law on International Arbitration, and UNCITRAL Notes on Organizing Arbitral Proceedings.

The court should be established by international treaty, which is basically an agreement between parties on the international scene. The term 'treaty' itself is the one most used in the context of international agreements, but there are a variety of titles that can and sometimes are used to express the same concept, such as protocol, act, charter, covenant, pact and concordat.

Structure of the court

The court could be composed of not more than five arbitrators from both the debtor and creditor sides, with an independent arbitrator to ensure impartiality. This kind of composition has been used in other arbitral tribunals. However, such a court could also maintain a panel of arbitrators from which parties can choose. It would have a secretariat to provide the necessary organizational support. Existing facilities such as courtrooms, a library, and consultation rooms belonging to the PCA in the Hague could be accessed.

Stay of proceedings

It is a common feature of court and arbitral proceedings for parties to apply for stay of proceedings pending disposal of arbitral proceedings. Under this power, repayment of particular disputed loans could be frozen, stayed or suspended until the court makes a decision. This power may be vested in the court by treaty and the rules of the court. The idea is to maintain the status quo until an action is disposed of.

THE QUESTION OF A GLOBAL DEBT TREATY

After the Second World War and the founding of the Federal Republic of Germany, the latter found itself with such a burden of debts, variously disputed in detail, that they stood in the way of establishing normal commercial relations in the international field. These debts comprised liability under the Treaty of Versailles (as modified by the Dawes and Young Plans); Second World War liabilities towards victors and other states; debts due on bonds issued by Germany; and private debts from the period prior to the two world wars.

As a result of the work of the Tripartite Commission on German Debts (established in 1951) and the London Debt Conference of 1952, and further negotiations at government level, the London Agreement on German External Debts was concluded on 27 February 1953. Pursuant to the London Debt Agreement, various arbitral tribunals were established with mandates to deal with German debts owed to foreign countries. The Mixed Graeco-German Arbitral Tribunal dealt with Greek debt claims against Germany; the Mixed German-American Commission was also mandated to handle claims made by Americans against Germany.

These arbitral tribunals determined claims and disputes relating to Germany's foreign debts as and when these arose between Germany and any of its creditors. Thus, in Greece vs. Federal Republic of Germany, the issue to be determined by the arbitral tribunal was whether or not, given the London Agreement, Greece and Germany were under an obligation to negotiate concerning the dispute in terms of the 'inclusive amounts' principles laid down in the Dawes Plan and replaced by the Young Plan; if Germany was liable to make certain payments to Greece on account of awards made by the Mixed Graeco-German Arbitration Tribunal; and to what end the obligation to negotiate was to be understood.

The underlying rationale of both the London Debt Conference and the establishment of the various arbitral bodies to deal with questions relating to German foreign debt was to restore the credit worthiness of the heavily indebted German Republic as an economic partner to the European Allied Powers and the USA. The ascertainment of Germany's total debt was necessary so that a redemption schedule could be worked out which Germany could adhere to without endangering its economy and its currency. Thus, more than merely settling disputes, the various tribunals established under the London Debt Agreement also functioned as fact-finding bodies.

The approach and rationale adopted by the victors after the two world wars regarding German foreign debts can be adopted mutatis mutandis in respect of the foreign debts of countries in the developing world. The process of consultation that culminated in the London Debt Conference, plus the outcomes of the conference itself, are definitely useful and can be modified and adopted for third world debt. An intergovernmental conference on third world debt may result in the adoption of a Multilateral Agreement on Indebted States (MAIS), which could serve as the framework agreement for working out country-specific solutions to the debt problem. Unlike the HIPC initiative, this will be more broadly based and the terms and conditions of debt relief or cancellation/forgiveness would not be imposed upon developing countries by IFIs.

Arbitral tribunals established pursuant to the MAIS should also be vested with broad powers to investigate and determine questions of fact and law relating to debts contracted by third world countries, the impact of debt servicing on economic performance (especially its impact on the country's ability to provide basic services such as health, education and food) and the extent to which debt servicing undermines fundamental human rights generally. Such tribunals should also have the power to decide matters relating to the conditions under which the debt was contracted, so as to determine whether there are any vitiating factors - duress, undue influence and violation of public policy - that may occasion the discharge of the indebted country from its debt obligations.

Implications for Long-term Global Governance and the Role of the UN

Establishing a court of arbitration under United Nations auspices has several advantages. It will immediately confer on the court a higher level of acceptability and legitimacy than would probably be the case without the support of the UN. Also, the UN has a pool of resources - human, financial and logistical - that the court can immediately rely upon to commence operations. These resources may be difficult to mobilize outside the framework of the UN system. It is also the case that the UN has a better institutional memory of the history, magnitude and developmental implications of southern indebtedness than any other organization in the world. This would be useful for dispute resolution.

Should the UN become involved in assisting states to resolve debt by arbitration, it should be very careful to avoid being seen as partisan to either borrowers or lenders. It is conceivable that the UN (or a suitable agency of the UN) might play the role of mediator in debt issues, or provide official mediators to assist parties to resolve debt problems, before submission to the costly and risky process of arbitration is necessary. This may enhance the UN's image and its role.

One course of action for the UN would be to sponsor an assessment of debt and its implications. Such an assessment could be followed with technical advice and assistance to states on both sides of the debt divide. However, depending on the outcome of assessment, this may be a difficult role for the UN to play and still maintain its neutrality. Alienation of lenders or debtors would impinge negatively on the UN. For that reason, the court of arbitration could be set up on the basis of a treaty. Another option would be for the African Union (in the case of Africa) to take up the assessment, as well as speak on behalf of African nations.

The 'moral hazard' dilemma

The United Nations framework is important for working towards a treaty and its ratification. In view of the fact that creditors have been reluctant to hold an international conference on debt, third world countries (with the assistance of other progressive countries and the UN secretary general) will have to work towards such a treaty or treaties on the debt of sovereign states and/or the issue of corruption. A convention dealing with money stolen by corrupt state officials could similarly establish the principles that apply to its tracking and return.

State parties to any such convention or treaty could agree to submit future disputes to binding arbitration, conducted with reference to the principles detailed in the convention or treaty and under the auspices of an identified and suitable arbitral organization, such as the PCA. A General Assembly Resolution on these issues may find support and aid in the general success of any such treaty or convention.

However extensive research into existing international law and surveys of state opinion on such a resolution, a convention or treaty would naturally be necessary and would be best conducted by the UN itself; in particular, by the International Law Commission (ILC) of the UN.

Implications of the Arbitration Mechanism for Development Cooperation

Permitting heavily indebted states to avoid payment of debts, or forgiving a debt or portion of a debt on a large scale, raises the 'moral hazard' for lenders that their debtors will not view any debt as repayable and will begin large-scale repudiations. Equally, a moral hazard for borrowers comes into play with reckless, illegitimate, invalid and irresponsible lending which results in unpayable debt. Both of these undermine the viability of the international financial system and should therefore be eliminated as part of the new international financial architecture.

The challenge of the debt of states on the basis of legal and other principles such as equity and human rights, through the arbitration mechanism, will play a role in reshaping the relationship between lender and borrower, and civil society will benefit from improved outcomes of loan resources.

A well-conceived and well-designed dispute settlement mechanism certainly has the potential for improving development cooperation between developed and developing countries. In the view of some policy-makers from developing countries, development assistance means little in the face of debts that virtually 'strangulate' the economies of developing countries. A mechanism for dispute settlement that can ensure that debt is not an obstacle to economic development is certain to improve the relations of developed and developing countries in the development process. Thus, a dispute settlement mechanism established with broad support from both creditor and debtor countries could drastically improve North-South development cooperation.

Inclusion of arbitration clauses in loan agreements

It is suggested that debtor states push for the inclusion of appropriate arbitration clauses in future loan agreements. Should an appropriate arbitration framework be identified or engineered, such a clause should make reference to the framework. The clause may make reference to a staged dispute resolution procedure, starting with negotiation and proceeding to mediation and arbitration as necessary. However, as what is appropriate may vary, specific legal advice should be taken in each instance. Arbitration centres may be in a position to assist or to suggest experts who can help in this regard.

Conclusion

The real question that remains is what mechanism should be established. This should be a subject of further discussion and will be pursued with the United Nations. Our current position is that an international arbitration mechanism on debt should be established. A court is long overdue, but use of existing institutions could be acceptable if it tackled the specific and unique aspects of the debt crisis.

2

Efficacy of Introducing an International Arbitration Court for Debt

African Forum and Network on Debt and Development

INTRODUCTION

The United Nations Charter on Human Rights, the African Charter on Human and People's Rights, and the Arusha Charter on Popular Participation compel us to claim that human development should not be compromised by international power imbalances in favour of rich creditor nations and institutions against severely indebted low-income countries, their governments and their peoples.

The persistence of the current debt crisis compromises human development in debt-burdened countries and is a reflection of the power imbalance and lack of political will on the part of rich nations and their institutions. It also reflects the lack of fair and democratic global governance that would of necessity lead to debt cancellation and tangible debt relief against dubious, unpayable, odious and illegitimate debts.

This chapter discusses the efficacy of establishing an international arbitration court to deal specifically with the special case of the debt crisis. It is our sincere hope and trust that it provides some ground for action to be undertaken under the auspices of the United Nations.

It is common knowledge that many least-developed countries are overburdened with foreign debts which they are unable to pay. The debt crisis has in fact compromised human development, especially in Africa and other less developed regions. While creditor governments and institutions continue to claim that adequate relief will be secured through the Heavily Indebted Poor Countries initiative (HIPC), debtor nations contend that creditors are not meeting their international obligations and commitments to resolve the debt crisis.

It is also recognized that many low-income countries have accumulated debts and now face servicing obligations that constrain their ability to support poverty reduction programmes, including those aimed at fulfilling basic human needs and financing critical growth-oriented investments.

The UN secretary general's December 2000 Report on the Financing for Development Process noted that while the need remains for clearer principles and more transparent mechanisms for working out debt problems under the Paris Club (a creditor organization), new and complementary approaches may be required. The basic fact broadly remains that existing mechanisms do not adequately and satisfactorily address debt issues. In particular, there are no neutral, fair and transparent globally binding arbitration mechanisms between debtors and creditors that would enable debtors to seek redress in cases of unpayable or illegitimate debts. Creditors prescribe initiatives and make rules designed to serve their own interests. They also make all the decisions, define the rules of borrowing and repayment and impose their own tailor-made measures through the Bretton Woods institutions and the like. The Paris Club, for example, is an undemocratic institution, which can be equated to a gang of creditors acting against one debtor. These undemocratic practices ought to be replaced with structures that respect human rights, democracy and the right of debtor countries and their people to be heard. Institutions should be put in place that are based on global consensus and aimed at safeguarding the interests of all, as well as building consensus based on respect for human rights and other aspirations enshrined in the United Nations Charter.

The real workable option for tackling the debt crisis and the problems highlighted above is an international legal process of arbitration that preserves the integrity of debtor countries and ensures that creditors share the responsibility for the failure of the development process and the rise of the debt crisis. Such a solution should also not undermine the long-term development prospects of debtor countries. The arbitration process should introduce a more neutral approach to an ongoing process of removing the debt burden. This approach would be a departure from the existing debt relief process, which is based on favouritism or the strategic importance of the debtor country in terms of the military, foreign policy or economic interests of creditor countries. The introduction of an international arbitration court on debt has been proposed as a way of tackling the problem.

INTERNATIONAL COMMERCIAL ARBITRATION GENERALLY

The arbitral process

In order to establish an independent international arbitration court to preside over and solve debt payment problems between sovereign debtors and creditors, as well as make decisions on unpayable, dubious and illegitimate debts, a suitable legal framework should be put in place. What type of legal framework would be appropriate for such an institution? In order to answer this question, it is important firstly to examine the concept of international commercial arbitration and such related concepts as negotiation, mediation and conciliation.

Issues of lending, borrowing and debt generally fall within the realm of international commercial arbitration. Arbitration is one of the alternative methods of resolving disputes outside the traditional court system. According to Halsbury's *Laws of England* (vol. 2, para 601: 332–3):

> Arbitration is the process by which a dispute or difference between two or more parties as to their mutual rights and liabilities are referred to and determined judicially and with binding effect by the application of law by one or more persons (the arbitral tribunal), instead of by a court of law. The decision of the arbitral tribunal is usually called an award. The reference to arbitration may arise from the agreement of the parties (private arbitration) or from statute. The agreement of the parties is in practice almost invariably in writing.

The term 'award' refers to the decision of the arbitrator, as opposed to the term 'judgement' used in the court. In this context an arbitrator can even deliver an interim or partial award. This definition of arbitration summarizes the elements of arbitration, as it is understood at common law.

Arbitration is the favoured method for settling international business disputes. Agreements to arbitrate are commonly found in international contracts for the sale of goods, the transfer of technology, and the undertaking of foreign investments. Arbitration is an ancient method of dispute resolution common to most cultures. Today, international arbitration is widespread and many arbitration centres are established. While it has numerous variations, arbitration is basically a method of dispute resolution whereby the parties to a dispute submit their conflict to a third person and agree to be bound by that person's decision. The arbitrator decides the matter in a rational and principled way and gives each party an opportunity to be heard. The jurisdictional basis of arbitration resides in the agreement by the parties to submit their disputes to the arbitral process. Without such agreement, the parties cannot be compelled to submit to arbitration, and any resulting arbitral award can be successfully attacked by showing that an agreement to arbitrate was absent or defective. In international business, agreements to arbitrate take one of two forms:

1. A provision – usually referred to as an arbitration clause – in a contract, stipulating that future disputes arising under or in connection with the contract are to be submitted to arbitration.
2. An agreement – usually called a submission agreement – by which the parties to a specific existing dispute agree to submit that dispute to arbitration.

International commercial arbitration is highly complex because numerous arbitral systems for international business disputes exist throughout the world.

Arbitration procedure

It must be stressed that arbitration is a principled and rational method of dispute resolution which seeks to arrive at a result on the basis of the evidence and the arguments presented to the arbitral panel. It is by no means a form of conciliation, mediation or negotiation. Although an arbitral proceeding may not exhibit the procedural technicalities common to judicial hearings, it must nevertheless conform to minimal standards of justice common to most of the world's legal systems. Indeed, the failure to respect minimal requirements of justice may mean that a court of law will refuse to enforce any resulting arbitral award. Thus, the parties must be given an opportunity to be heard, the arbitrator must be impartial, and the decision-making process must be fair.

The arbitral process, like a court case, proceeds in a series of definite procedural stages. Thus, the aggrieved party must initiate the process by filing a demand for arbitration, which the respondent must answer. The arbitrator or arbitrators must then be selected and their powers defined. The time and place of the arbitration hearing must be determined, along with the appropriate procedure. At the hearing, each side submits its evidence, and the parties have the opportunity to argue their individual cases. Based on the evidence, the argument of the parties, and the applicable rules and principles, the arbitrators decide on the dispute and prepare an award embodying their decision.

Although the stages of arbitration are fairly uniform throughout the world, the requirements and rules applicable to each stage may differ significantly among the various arbitration systems. The procedural rules applicable to a given arbitration depend essentially on the will of the parties. Most commonly, the arbitration agreement will contain a provision adopting an entire body of rules promulgated by an institution such as the International Chamber of Commerce (ICC), the American Arbitration Association (AAA), or the United Nations Commission on International Trade Law (UNCITRAL) rules. To supplement or to replace these rules, the parties may also define special rules to apply to their arbitration. Most legal systems will respect such procedures unless they are fundamentally unfair or are the product of fraud or overreaching. Indeed, failure of the arbitral tribunal to follow the procedures stipulated by the parties may be grounds for invalidating any eventual award.

If the parties have not specified a particular rule or if the adopted set of rules is silent on the matter, the arbitral tribunal is normally competent to establish the procedures for the arbitration. Generally speaking, arbitration rules are not as well defined and detailed as a court's procedural rules. Moreover, little precedent exists to assist arbitrators in understanding and applying existing rules such as those promulgated by the ICC or UNCITRAL. The arbitrator therefore has significant discretion to shape the procedure applicable to the arbitration.

The arbitration agreement may also specify the law applicable to the arbitration. International law may also be applied in settling disputes through arbitration.

Appointment or selection of arbitrators

In international commercial arbitration the appointment of an arbitral tribunal, panel of arbitrators or a single arbitrator is a matter for negotiation between the parties, with each side generally appointing one or more 'national' arbitrators and the remaining 'neutral' members being agreed between them. If the parties can settle the composition of the tribunal at an early stage it will be possible to name the members in the arbitration agreement. Frequently, however, the identity of the members is left to be settled later, in which case the agreement will simply define the membership of the tribunal and lay down the procedure to be followed in setting it up.

For obvious reasons, the result of a panel of arbitrators often turns on the decisions of the neutral member or members. Deciding who they shall be is therefore extremely important to the parties concerned, who may sometimes find it difficult to agree on suitable candidates. To take account of this, arbitration agreements or treaties often provide that in the event of disagreement the neutral members may be appointed by the president of an international arbitral institution such as the Permanent Court of Arbitration (PCA) or by some other disinterested party.

Effect of an award

An arbitral award is binding, but not necessarily final in certain instances, for it may be open to parties to take further proceedings to interpret, revise, rectify, appeal from or nullify the decision. Whether such steps are permissible, and if so, whether the new case can be heard by the original tribunal, or must be brought before another tribunal or body, depends partly on general international law, but mainly on the terms of the arbitration agreement.

The power to interpret an award, or to appeal against it, must normally be the subject of an express agreement. Since the object of the parties in going to arbitration is to end the dispute, provisions for appeal are relatively rare. Interpretation, on the other hand, which concerns the clarification of an award, not its correctness, is easier to justify and more commonly allowed.

An award may also be set aside on some restricted grounds. Grounds for setting aside are restricted because parties take cases to arbitration with the intention of obtaining a decision which both parties will be bound to carry out and which will put an end to the dispute. But a decision is only binding in international law if the tribunal has been properly constituted, has carried out its instructions and has produced an adequate award. It is therefore possible for a party to deny that an award is effective by invoking the doctrine of nullity.

Again, an arbitrator has no jurisdiction to give an award if the instrument from which they claim to derive their authority is invalid, not yet in force or has terminated. It is also possible to dispute an award on the basis that the arbitrator's appointment was not in accordance with the agreement.

An award may also be set aside on grounds of fraud or if it is contrary to public policy.

Enforcement of the arbitral award

Once the arbitrator had rendered an award, the winning party then faces the problem of securing its enforcement. Unlike the judge in a court of law, an arbitrator does not have the power to compel a party to obey the award. In order to obtain respect for the award in the face of opposition by the losing side, the winning party must bring into play the coercive power of the state through its legal and judicial systems. In many cases, of course, enforcement problems do not arise because the parties, having agreed to arbitration in the first place, are willing to abide by the arbitrator's decision. Indeed, it has been claimed that 90 per cent of awards made by the ICC are respected by the parties, without the need for judicial enforcement measures. Numerous business reasons may lead a losing party to obey the arbitral award despite the fact that no court has compelled them to do so. For example, if confidentiality was an important factor in selecting arbitration as a means of dispute resolution in the first place, the losing party might not wish to become embroiled in a judicial enforcement proceeding that would make the dispute a matter of public record. Also, if arbitration is a normal procedure in a particular trade or business, a losing party's lack of respect for the award might be viewed negatively by other persons in the trade and thus damage that party's business reputation.

Despite the high percentage of awards that are respected by the parties without recourse to judicial enforcement, the attorney planning for international business dispute resolution must nonetheless take into account the possibility of being required to seek judicial enforcement of an arbitral award. Indeed, planning for future arbitration requires the attorney to seek two competing goals:

1 quick and efficacious enforcement of the award should a client win the arbitration;
2 protection in the courts from the results of an unfair arbitral proceeding should they lose.

First, if his or her client wins the arbitration, the attorney will naturally wish to enforce the resulting award as quickly and efficiently as possible, either in the country in which the award was rendered or in any other country in which the losing party has property that may be used to satisfy the award. The enforcement of an arbitral award in any country depends on the domestic law of that country. The law on the enforcement of arbitral awards is therefore specific to each country; however, as will be seen below, significant progress toward the establishment of commonly accepted legal principles on this subject has been made in the last few decades and incorporated into the legal systems of many countries through international treaties providing for the enforcement of foreign arbitral awards.

Obviously, the ideal situation for any winning party is that any court in the world will recognize and enforce an award as final and binding with a minimum of procedural technicalities. Since the purpose of selecting arbitration in the first place is to avoid the use of the courts and the resulting expense and delay, it would defeat the purpose of that choice if, after obtaining an award, the winning party had to spend considerable time and resources in the courts to enforce it so as to obtain a meaningful satisfaction of the claim. Clearly, what the winning party in an arbitration wishes to avoid at all costs is the necessity of relitigating *de novo* the claim before a judge. Thus, in planning for arbitration, it is important that the attorney bear in mind enforcement problems.

On the other hand, parties planning for arbitration also want assurance that they will receive fair treatment in the arbitral proceeding and that, if they do not, they will have the possibility of protecting their legal rights in the courts. Some treaties have sought to facilitate the enforcement of arbitral awards. The lack of an appropriate treaty will mean that the winning party must rely purely on the vagaries of local law, which may or may not favour the recognition and enforcement of foreign awards.

In an effort to facilitate the enforcement of international commercial arbitral awards, various nations of the world have concluded treaties, the purpose of which is to create binding legal obligations to recognize and enforce such awards. One of the earliest such multilateral treaties was the Geneva Convention for the Execution of Foreign Arbitral Awards, signed in 1927. The approximately twenty countries that ratified the Geneva Convention did not include the United States. After the Second World War, the expansion of international business gave a new impetus to efforts to create a global framework for the enforcement of international commercial arbitration awards. This effort culminated in the New York Convention on the Recognition and Enforcement of Foreign Arbitral Awards, concluded in 1958.

The next section is devoted principally to a consideration of the New York Convention's provisions, for it has become the legal basis for award enforcement throughout much of the world. Certain other relevant treaties affecting the enforcement of arbitral awards are also mentioned.

Enforcement under the New York Convention

The New York Convention was the result of a diplomatic conference held at the United Nations between 20 May and 10 June 1958, when the representatives of 45 nations met to establish a basic international framework for the recognition of arbitral agreements and the enforcement of arbitral awards. Although the United States attended the conference, it did not ratify the Convention immediately because of fears of possible conflict between the provisions of the Convention and certain United States laws. Ultimately, under pressure from the American business community and adherence to the Convention by major US treaty partners, the United States ratified the Convention, and Congress amended the US Arbitration Act to provide for its enforcement. The New York Convention became effective in the United States on 29 December 1970.

The ability of a party to obtain the benefit of the UN Convention for purposes of enforcing an arbitral award in the courts of a particular country will depend on whether that country is a party to the Convention. As of 21 May 1996, 108 countries had ratified the New York Convention. While the parties to the Convention include major US trading partners, as well as the Soviet Union and many Eastern European countries, it should be noted that most Latin American states have refused to participate. It should also be noted that many countries have adhered to the Convention with specific reservations and that the existence of such reservations may affect an attorney's ability to invoke the treaty provisions in a particular case. Article 1 (3) of the convention provides that any ratifying state may establish either or both of the following two reservations:

1. That the ratifying state will apply the Convention to the recognition and enforcement of awards made only in the territory of another contracting state.
2. That it will apply the Convention only to differences arising out of legal relationships, whether contractual or not, which are considered as commercial under the national law of the state making such reservation.

In acceding to the Convention, the United States specifically adopted both reservations.

Although the goal of the Convention has been to develop a globally uniform law on the enforcement of arbitral awards, and although it has succeeded in this regard to a remarkable extent, the provisions of the Convention, as part of local law, have been subject to interpretation and application by national courts. Such interpretations may vary on certain points from country to country. A useful publication which follows the judicial decisions under the Convention is the *Yearbook Commercial Arbitration* (Deventer, the Netherlands), published by the International Council for Commercial Arbitration. This annual publication, which begun in 1976, reports on judicial decisions from numerous jurisdictions.

Since procedural rules governing the enforcement of arbitral awards remain within the discretion of individual states, such rules, in addition to divergent interpretations of the Convention's provisions, may also influence the practical application of the Convention in a given country.

Defences to the enforcement of an award under the Convention

The fundamental objective of the Convention is to facilitate the recognition and enforcement of awards, and it therefore imposes an affirmative obligation upon the contracting state parties to recognize and enforce such awards. The Convention itself makes no provision whatsoever for the setting aside of awards; however, it does recognize that the arbitral process may have been so tainted or abusive as to make any resulting award invalid and therefore unenforceable. In order to protect parties from illegal and abusive arbitral processes, the Convention establishes a specific list of defences, which the defendant may raise in an enforcement action in order to prevent the enforcement of an award. In this regard, the Convention defines seven grounds, which, if established, will justify a court in refusing to enforce an award. The first five grounds, set out in Article 5 (1), place the burden of proof upon the party opposing enforcement. The last two grounds, defined in Article 5 (2), may be raised by the court on its own motion. Each of these seven defences are considered in turn below. The seven grounds listed in the Convention are exhaustive: a court may not refuse to enforce an arbitral award for other reasons.

Invalidity of the arbitration agreement

Article 5 (1) states that recognition and enforcement of the award may be refused, at the request of the party against whom it is invoked, only if that party furnishes to the competent authority where the recognition and enforcement is sought, proof that:

> The parties to the agreement referred to in Article 2 were, under the law applicable to them, under some incapacity or the said agreement is not valid under the law to which the parties have subjected it or, failing any indication thereon, under the law of the country where the award was made.

Violation of due process

The second ground specified in Article 5 relates generally to a violation of due process or fairness in the arbitral proceedings. According to its terms, recognition may be refused if 'the party against whom the award is invoked was not given proper notice of the appointment of the arbitrator or of the arbitration proceedings or was otherwise unable to present his case.' Clearly, the purpose of this provision is to provide sufficient notice to the opposing party so as to enable them to participate meaningfully in the arbitration proceeding.

Excess authority by the arbitrator

Under Article 5 (1) (c), a court may refuse to enforce an award which decides issues outside the scope of the arbitrator's authority. Thus, the Convention provides that if 'the award deals with a difference not contemplated by or not falling within the terms of the submission to arbitration, or it contains decisions on matters beyond the scope of the submission to arbitrate', then it cannot be enforced. If the arbitrator exceeds the authority on certain issues and not on others, such action does not nullify the entire award. Article 5 (1) (c) contains the provision 'that, if the decision on matters submitted to arbitration can be separated from those not so submitted, that part of the award which contains decisions on matters submitted to arbitration may be recognized and enforced.'

Irregularity in the composition of the arbitral tribunal or the arbitral procedure
Under this defence, the court may refuse enforcement of the award if 'the composition of the arbitral tribunal or the arbitral procedure was not in accordance with the agreement of the parties, or failing such agreement, was not in accordance with the law of the country where the arbitration took place.'

For example, if the arbitration agreement provided for a three-person arbitral panel but the award was rendered by a sole arbitrator, such an award could be challenged under Article 5 of the Convention. Similarly, if the parties agreed to the application of UNCITRAL rules, and the arbitrator applied ICC rules, such action would also constitute a reason for refusing enforcement of an award.

Award not binding or set aside or suspended
The final ground stipulated in paragraph 1 of Article 5 provides that a court may refuse to enforce an award if 'the award has not yet become binding on the parties, or had been set aside or suspended by the competent authority in the country in which, or under the law of which, that award was made.'

Thus, if a court in a country in which the award is made sets the award aside, the courts in other countries are not obligated to enforce it.

Other Treaties
Since most of the world's principal trading countries are parties to the New York Convention, it constitutes the most important legal basis for the enforcement of arbitration awards in international business today. Many countries, particularly in Latin America, are not yet parties to the Convention. In dealing with such countries, other international agreements relating to the enforcement of arbitration awards may exist as aids to enforcement, and the international business attorney ought to be aware of them, for they may have applicability where the New York Convention does not apply or cannot apply. Moreover, in certain situations, even where the New York Convention does apply, such other treaties may offer more favourable conditions for enforcing an award; consequently, a winning party may prefer to invoke its provisions rather than those of the New York Convention. Such bilateral and multilateral treaties are mentioned briefly.

In order to provide a basis for enforcement of arbitration awards among European countries, the European Convention on International Commercial Arbitration was concluded at Geneva on 21 April 1961. It was subsequently modified by the Paris Agreement of 17 December 1962. As of 1984, 18 countries, including France, Germany, Italy and the USSR, had ratified the European Convention.

As noted earlier, relatively few Latin American states have ratified the New York Convention. Their opposition to the Convention is based largely on the Calvo doctrine and their unwillingness to yield the jurisdiction of their own courts to that of international tribunals. In an effort, nonetheless, to provide a workable system of international arbitration, the Latin American states have drafted the Inter-American Convention on International Commercial Arbitration of 1975. Although many of this Convention's provisions are similar to those of the New York Convention, there are certain important differences. For example, whereas the New York Convention requires that at the request of one of the parties to arbitration, a court takes action to the dispute subject to an arbitration agreement, the Inter-American Convention on International Commerical Arbitration is silent on this specific question. As a result, the issue of whether or not a court must refer the parties to arbitration would presumably be determined under the local law of each contracting party. In addition, whereas the New York Convention does not provide for rules of arbitral procedure, the Inter-American Convention requires that in the absence of an express agreement between the parties, the Inter-American Commercial Arbitration rules of procedure are to apply to the proceedings.

Bilateral treaties on economic and commercial relations sometimes contain references to arbitration and the enforcement of arbitral awards. The United States has entered into bilateral economic and commercial treaties with over forty different countries, and many of them specifically deal with the enforcement in one country of an arbitral award issued in another. The precise nature of such provision is subject to variation among US bilateral treaties.

Enforcement in the Absence of Treaty Provisions

Despite the absence of a relevant treaty, enforcement in one country of an arbitral award made in another may still be possible. In such cases, enforcement will depend exclusively on the law of the jurisdiction in which enforcement is sought. Some legal systems may allow enforcement of foreign awards without significant difficulties, while others may impose conditions, such as reciprocity with the awarding state, a de novo review by the enforcing courts, or the satisfaction of burdensome procedural requirements. Some countries, such as West Germany, have enacted specific legislative provisions governing the enforcement of foreign arbitral awards not subject to treaties or conventions. Others, like the United States, have no specific legislation on this topic. In the US, principles of comity govern the enforcement of arbitral awards.

NEGOTIATION, MEDIATION AND CONCILIATION

Negotiation

Disputes are inevitable both in international relations and in commercial investment transactions. When a government or institution anticipates that a decision or a proposed course of action may harm another state or institution, discussions with the affected party can provide a way of heading off a dispute by creating an opportunity for adjustment and accommodation. Consultations, discussions and negotiations are a valuable way of avoiding international disputes generally.

Negotiations between states are usually conducted through normal diplomatic channels; that is, by the respective foreign offices, or diplomatic representatives, who in the case of complex negotiations may lead delegations that include representatives of several interested departments of the governments concerned.

As an alternative, if the subject matter is appropriate, negotiations may be carried out by what are termed the 'competent authorities' of each party; that is, by representatives of the particular ministry or department responsible for the matter in question – between trade departments in the case of a commercial agreement, for example, or between defence ministries in negotiations concerning weapons procurement. Where the competent authorities are subordinate bodies, they may be authorized to take negotiations as far as possible and to refer disagreements to a higher governmental level.

Mediation

When the parties to an international dispute or domestic dispute are unable to resolve it by negotiation, the intervention of a third party is a possible means of breaking the impasse and producing an acceptable solution. Such intervention can take a number of different forms. The third party may simply encourage the disputing states to resume negotiations, or do nothing more than provide them with an additional channel of communication. In these situations they are said to be contributing their good offices. On the other hand, their job may be to investigate the dispute and to present the parties with a set of formal proposals for its solution. This form of intervention is called conciliation. Between good offices and conciliation lies the form of third-party activity known as mediation.

Like good offices, mediation is essentially an adjunct of negotiation, but with the mediator as an active participant, authorized and indeed expected to advance their own proposals and to interpret, as well as to transmit, each party's proposals to the other. What distinguishes this kind of assistance from conciliation is that a mediator generally makes proposals informally and on the basis of information supplied by the parties, rather than his or her own investigations, although in practice such distinctions tend to be blurred. In a given case it may therefore be difficult to draw the line between mediation and conciliation, or to say exactly when good offices ended and mediation began.

Mediation may be performed by international organizations, by states or by individuals. For the United Nations and a number of regional organizations, the settlement of disputes is a basic institutional objective and as a result the secretary general and his regional counterparts are often engaged in providing good offices and mediation. In certain situations non-governmental organizations (NGOs) can act as mediators. The International Committee of the Red Cross (ICRC), for example, avoids involvement in political disputes, but regularly intervenes where armed conflict or the treatment of detainees raise humanitarian issues. Since it offers the opportunity to become involved in a dispute and to influence its outcome, the role of mediator also has attractions for states concerned to see a dispute resolved peacefully or amicably, or with an interest in a particular solution. Thus, it is not unusual to find the course of an international dispute punctuated by offers of mediation from one or more outside parties.

Mediation cannot be forced on the parties to an international dispute, but only takes place if they consent. So unless they have taken the initiative and appointed a mediator already, their unwillingness to consider this form of assistance may prove a major stumbling block. This is because although a mediator's proposals are not binding, the very act of mediation has implications, which may be unacceptable to either or both of the governments concerned.

If mediation becomes possible when the parties suspect that a settlement on their own terms may no longer be achievable at an acceptable cost, then the mediator's task is to devise or promote a solution from which both can derive a measure of satisfaction. This may, of course, be impossible, in which case mediation will fail. But resourceful mediators have a variety of means at their disposal to avoid this result. They can do much by simply providing good offices and facilitating communication between the parties. If a dispute is serious enough to call for the services of a mediator, it is possible that events have already had the effect of restricting the parties' contact, or have made it difficult for them to deal with each other openly.

Conciliation

Conciliation has been defined as:

> A method for the settlement of international disputes of any nature according to which a Commission set up by the Parties, either on a permanent basis or an ad hoc basis to deal with a dispute, proceeds to the impartial examination of the dispute and attempts to define the terms of a settlement susceptible of being accepted by them or of affording the Parties, with a view to its settlement, such aid as they may have requested. (Article 1 of the Regulations on the Procedure of International Conciliation, adopted by the Institute of International Law in 1961)

The eclectic character of the method is at once apparent. If mediation is essentially an extension of negotiation, conciliation puts third-party intervention on a formal legal footing and institutionalizes it in a way comparable, but not identical, to inquiry or arbitration. For the fact-finding exercise that is the essence of inquiry may or may not be an important element in conciliation, while the search for terms susceptible of being accepted by the parties, but not binding on them, provides a sharp contrast with arbitration and a reminder of the link between conciliation and mediation.

All conciliation commissions have the same functions: to investigate the dispute and to suggest the terms of a possible settlement. However, within this broad mandate, conciliation commissions have performed a variety of different tasks. What a commission does and how it goes about its work depends in the first place on the instrument setting it up. But much also depends on how the parties choose to present the particular case, and whether members of the commission exhibit many common features or significant differences of approach to most basic matters.

What sort of process is conciliation? One view is that it is to be regarded as a kind of institutionalized negotiation. The task of the commission is to encourage and structure the parties' dialogue, while providing them with whatever assistance may be necessary to bring it to a successful conclusion. This approach, which proceeds from the premise that the resolution of disputes depends on securing the parties' agreement, finds an affinity between conciliation and mediation. Another view is that conciliation is close to inquiry or arbitration; that the commission's function is to provide information and advice as to the merits of the parties' position and to suggest a settlement that corresponds to what they deserve, not what they claim.

ESTABLISHMENT OF AN INTERNATIONAL ARBITRATION COURT ON DEBT

Justification for such a court

Having examined the various alternative mechanisms of settling disputes, there is no doubt that arbitration stands out as the most appropriate mode of resolving commercial disputes. As seen above, arbitration has been popularized and used extensively in the settlement of commercial disputes. The same mode of resolving disputes can be utilized for commercial disputes concerning debt. The other modes of dispute resolution – negotiation, mediation and conciliation – may also be fused in the court's legal framework for resolving disputes, depending on the nature and complexity of each dispute.

The unique problem of debt calls for the establishment of a special court. Many arbitral institutions in the world do not restrict their modes of settling disputes to one mode. They employ methods and processes appropriate for each particular dispute. It would not be appropriate to enhance current mechanisms such as the Paris Club by introducing arbitration panels to hear possible disputes between debtors and creditors, as such a club (which is in fact a cartel) can still intimidate debtors under the guise of debt negotiation. The imbalances in bargaining power between creditors and debtors demand the establishment of a neutral and impartial arbitral institution.

The establishment of a unique arbitral institution to deal with the problem of debt is further justified by the fact that similar institutions have already been set up to deal with unique problems; for example, the International Centre for Settlement of Investment Disputes (ICSID) and the PCA. These institutions are analysed below.

ICSID

Foreign investment disputes between foreign investors and host country governments raise special problems; consequently, the normal mechanisms of international business dispute settlement may not be appropriate. A foreign investment dispute usually involves the government of the host country and is invariably highly political. Governments who have nationalized or otherwise interfered with a foreign investment project usually assert that their actions have been taken in the national interest and are a legitimate exercise of national sovereignty. As a result, foreign governments may be reluctant to conclude an arbitration agreement to submit future disputes concerning an investment project to normal international commercial arbitration, such as the ICC, which are, after all, institutions of private law. Indeed, the host government may argue that disputes arising out of expropriation or nationalization are not 'commercial' in nature and, therefore, are clearly outside the ambit of international commercial arbitration. Moreover, it may fear that institutions such as the ICC have a bias or an orientation toward private enterprise and are therefore unable to view the claims of a government with total neutrality. In addition, even if a government should agree to submit future disputes to arbitration, experience has shown that it is difficult to enforce such agreements against a government and even more difficult to enforce any resulting arbitration award.

At the same time, a foreign investor may be unwilling to rely solely on host country courts for protection in the event of a dispute with the government, since they may be subject to local political pressures. Normally, the investor would prefer an independent, neutral tribunal to secure enforcement of commitments and obligations made by a foreign government. The lack of such assurance may, of course, inhibit the investment from taking place and thus reduce the international flow of capital, particularly to less developed countries.

In the early 1960s the staff of the World Bank concluded that an institution designed to take account of the special problems of settling investment disputes between foreign private investors and host country governments would encourage the flow of needed capital to the developing world. In 1962 the board of governors of the Bank requested the executive directors to study the matter. After a series of discussions within the Bank, as well as meetings with legal experts in various parts of the world, the staff recommended that an international convention be prepared to establish an institution which would provide arbitration and conciliation facilities to settle such investment disputes. In 1964 the board of governors of the Bank directed the executive directors to 'formulate a convention establishing facilities and procedures which would be available on a voluntary basis for the settlement of investment disputes between contracting states and nationals of other contracting states through conciliation and arbitration.'

By 1965, the executive directors and the staff had completed their work in the form of the Convention on the Settlement of Investment Disputes between States and Nationals of other States, which was then submitted for approval to the member states of the World Bank. The Convention has steadily gained approval since that time. As of August 2001, 134 countries had ratified the Convention. Thus, it has received broad acceptance from the world community. Only two of the Latin American states, Paraguay and El Salvador, have ratified the Convention, a situation which is no doubt due to the Calvo doctrine and Latin America's traditional reluctance to accept international arbitration. Zambia is a signatory to the Convention and has incorporated it into its domestic laws by virtue of the Investment Disputes Convention Act, Chapter 42 of the Laws of Zambia. The United States ratified the Convention in 1966, and it entered into force in the United States as of 14 October 1966.

The International Centre for the Settlement of Investment Disputes

The Convention on the Settlement of Investment Disputes between States and Nationals of other States (sometimes referred to as the Washington Convention) creates an international institution in the form of the International Centre for the Settlement of Investment Disputes to provide facilities for conciliation and arbitration of investment disputes. Located in Washington, DC at the headquarters of the World Bank, from which it receives administrative and financial support, the centre itself does not engage in conciliation or arbitration; rather, it facilitates the establishment of arbitral tribunals and conciliation commissions in accordance with the provisions of the Convention. The centre's governing body, the administrative council, is composed of one representative of each contracting state. The ex-officio chairman of the administrative council is the president of the World Bank. The centre's principal executive officer, responsible for its day-to-day administration, is the secretary general, appointed by a two-thirds majority of the members of the administrative council and serving for a renewable term not exceeding six years.

One of the principal tasks of the centre is to maintain a panel of conciliators and a panel of arbitrators. Under Article 13 of the Convention, each contracting party may designate four persons to each panel. Such persons may, but need not be, nationals of the contracting state which nominates them. In addition, the chairperson may designate ten persons to each panel, provided that such persons each have a different nationality. Under Article 14, persons designated to serve on the panels are to have high moral character and recognized competence in the fields of law, commerce, industry or finance. They must also be relied upon to exercise independent judgement. Conciliators and arbitrators for actual investment disputes are to be drawn from these panels. The membership of the panels is a matter of public record and is normally published in ICSID's annual report.

Jurisdiction of the centre

The Convention was specifically designed to take account of the special characteristics of foreign investment disputes, as well as the special nature of the parties involved. It also seeks to maintain a careful balance between the interests of host states and the interests of investors. The precise nature of the balance is best illustrated in its jurisdictional provisions. Article 25 (1) of the Convention sets out the basic principle with respect to jurisdiction:

> The jurisdiction of the Centre shall extend to any legal dispute arising directly out of an investment, between a Contracting State (or any constituent subdivision or agency of a Contracting State designated to the Centre by that State) and a National of another Contracting State, which the parties to the dispute consent in writing to submit to the Centre. When the parties have given their consent, no party may withdraw its consent unilaterally.

Consent of the parties, as the report of the executive directors states, is the cornerstone of the centre's jurisdiction. Mere ratification of the Convention does not constitute sufficient consent to subject a contracting state to the jurisdiction of the centre for any and all future disputes. Rather, both the contracting state and the national of another contracting state must give their consent. Except to state that the consent must be in writing, the Convention does not specify the time at which consent should be given, nor the form it must take. Consent may be given, for example, in a clause included in an investment agreement, providing for the submission to the centre of future disputes arising out of that agreement, or in a compromise regarding a dispute which has already arisen.

The Convention gives no definition of the term 'investment'. Today, the concept of investment is, of course, very broad and may include arrangements beyond mere equity ownership, including management contracts, contracts for the sale and erection of industrial plants, turnkey contracts, and technology transfer agreements. Moreover, there is some indication that international loans to foreign sovereigns are beginning to include reference to ICSID arbitration as a way of meeting the opposition of certain powerful state borrowers to the standard loan provisions referring all disputes to the courts of the lender's home country.

It is important to note that once the parties have given consent, the Convention specifically provides that such consent may not be unilaterally withdrawn. If a party, having consented to ICSID arbitration, refuses to participate in the arbitral proceedings, the arbitration may proceed on an *ex parte* basis, and any resulting award will be enforceable as though the party had participated fully.

Arbitral proceedings under ICSID

The procedures and rules applicable to an ICSID arbitration are contained in its regulations and rules, which were first adopted by the ICSID administrative council in 1967, pursuant to Article 6 of the Convention.

A party may institute an arbitral proceeding by addressing a request to ICSID's secretary general, who then sends a copy to the other side. The request is to contain information concerning the issues in dispute, the identity of the parties, and their consent to arbitration in accordance with the Rules of Procedure for the Institution of Arbitration Proceedings. The secretary general is then to register the request, unless they find, on the basis of the information contained in the request, that the dispute is manifestly outside the jurisdiction of the centre. For example, if it is clear that the state in question is not a party to the Convention, the secretary general could refuse to register the dispute.

Once the request for arbitration has been registered, the arbitral tribunal is constituted as soon as possible. The tribunal consists of a sole arbitrator or any uneven number of arbitrators appointed in accordance with the parties' agreement. If the parties have not agreed upon the number of arbitrators and the method of their appointment, the Convention provides that the tribunal is to consist of three arbitrators, one appointed by each part and the third, who shall be the president of the tribunal, appointed by agreement of the parties. Under Article 30 of the Convention, the majority of the members of an arbitral tribunal should not ordinarily be nationals of either the state party to the dispute or the state whose national is a party to the dispute; however, this rule is not applicable if each and every arbitrator on the tribunal has been appointed by agreement of the parties. The Convention gives the parties flexibility in appointing arbitrators. They may appoint arbitrators from outside the panels of arbitrators maintained by the centre, but their appointees must possess the qualities, stated in Article 14, necessary for appointment to the centre's own panels. If the parties cannot agree upon the appointment of the arbitrator, or if one party refuses to proceed, the chairperson of ICSID, at the request of either party and after consulting both parties as far as possible, has the power to appoint the arbitrator or arbitrators not yet appointed. In making such selection the chairperson must choose arbitrators from the panels maintained by the centre, and must make such appointment within 90 days after notice of registration of the request.

ICSID arbitrations are to be conducted according to such rules as the parties have agreed upon; however, to the extent that they have not so agreed, the tribunal is to apply ICSID's own rules. In arriving at its decision, the arbitral tribunal is required to apply the law agreed by the parties. Failing such agreement, the tribunal must apply the law of the state party to the dispute (unless that law calls for the application of some other law), as well as such rules of international law as may be applicable. The Convention also aims to create a system of dispute settlement, which excludes control or scrutiny by the domestic courts of any state party. Thus, if a party who has agreed to ICSID arbitration nonetheless begins a suit in a domestic court, the court must stay the proceedings and refer the parties to ICSID arbitration. Similarly, if a party against whom a claim is brought in ICSID arbitration seeks to involve a court in reviewing ICSID procedure, such court ought to refrain from involving itself in that decision.

Within 60 days after the arbitral tribunal has been constituted, or such other period as the parties may agree, it meets for its first session. The arbitration proceedings are to be held at the seat of the centre, unless the parties have agreed to hold them at another place in accordance with Article 63 of the Convention. Moreover, the arbitration is to take place in private and remain secret. The arbitral proceeding consists of two distinct phases: a written procedure, followed by an oral one. During the written procedure, the parties file various pleadings, including a memorial by the requesting party, and a counter-memorial by the other party.

The oral procedure consists of the hearing by the tribunal of the parties, their agents, witnesses and experts. In hearing evidence, the tribunal is the judge of admissibility of any evidence adduced and of its probative value. If it deems it necessary, the tribunal may at any stage of the proceeding call upon the parties to produce documents, witnesses and experts, and it may visit or conduct inquiries at any place connected with the dispute. The parties are obligated to cooperate with the tribunal in the production of evidence, and the tribunal may take formal note of the failure of a party to comply with such obligations.

The award and its enforcement

When the parties have completed the presentation of their respective cases, the tribunal may declare the proceedings closed. Within 30 days after the closure of the proceedings, the tribunal should issue an award; however, it may extend this period by an additional 30 days. In making its award, the tribunal decides questions by a majority vote of all of its members. The award must be in writing and must be signed by all members of the tribunal who voted for it. In addition to the names of the parties, the award contains a summary of the proceedings, a statement of the facts as found by the tribunal, the submissions of the parties, the decision of the tribunal on every question submitted to it, together with the reasons upon which the decision is based, and any decision of the tribunal regarding the costs of the proceedings.

An award of an ICSID arbitral tribunal is binding between the parties and is not subject to any appeal or any remedy. Under Article 54 of the Convention, each contracting state is to recognize an ICSID award as binding and enforce the pecuniary obligations imposed by that award within its territories as if it were a final judgement of a court of that state. The enforcement provisions of the ICSID Convention are stronger than those of the 1958 New York Convention. Whereas the New York Convention contains certain specified defences to the enforcement of an arbitral award, including the defence of public policy, the ICSID Convention makes no provision for such defences. An ICSID award by the terms of the Convention is to be recognized and enforced as if it were a final judgement of a court in the enforcing state. In the event that a contracting state fails to abide by or to comply with an ICSID award, the Convention specifically provides that the contracting state whose national is a party to that award has the right to seek diplomatic protection and ultimately to bring an action against the offending state in the International Court of Justice.

ICSID is important, in that many international investment agreements include provision for submission to ICSID of investment disputes. In addition, many bilateral investment treaties also refer to ICSID in the event of an investment dispute. Generally speaking, such treaty provisions are of four types:

1. A general statement that if the parties to the dispute so agree, the dispute shall be referred to ICSID resolution. Such a provision, of course, requires that the necessary jurisdictional agreement be reached prior to submission to ICSID. The provision itself does not constitute such an agreement.
2. Certain treaties are somewhat stronger in stipulating that in the event of a dispute the state party will be receptive to a request by an injured investor to refer the dispute to ICSID.
3. Some treaties specifically contain an obligation by the host state to give its consent to ICSID arbitration at the request of the investor.
4. Several investment treaties include provisions which expressly stipulate that the host state thereby agrees to ICSID conciliation or arbitration.

The Permanent Court of Arbitration

The PCA is an international organization offering a broad range of services for resolving disputes between states, as well as disputes between states and private parties. These services include good offices and mediation, commissions of inquiry (fact finding), conciliation and arbitration. Established at the Hague by intergovernmental agreement in 1899 (revised in 1907), the PCA is the oldest institution dedicated to resolving international disputes. It has its offices in the Peace Palace in the Hague. The same building accommodates the International Court of Justice, the Hague Academy of International Law, and one of the most comprehensive and up-to-date international law libraries in the world.

The PCA has the status of a Permanent Observer at the United Nations General Assembly, and has a strong history of collaboration with the UN, reflecting the commitment of both organizations to the peaceful settlement of all types of international disputes.

Members of the court
The court consists of a panel of international jurists designated by the states parties to the Hague Convention of 1899 and/or 1907. From this panel the parties to a dispute may, if they so desire, select the members of a tribunal or commission to carry out the agreed-upon forum of dispute resolution. The 'members of the court' consist of over 260 potential arbitrators, all distinguished lawyers appointed by states parties to the Hague Conventions. The list of members of the court is published in the annual report of the administrative council.

International Bureau
The backbone of the PCA is its secretariat, which is known as the International Bureau. The International Bureau, headed by the secretary general, is responsible for the day to-day operations of the PCA, and serves as a registry in arbitrations conducted under its auspices. It also serves as its channel of communication (including communication between parties to proceedings administered by the Bureau) and maintains custody of its archives. It has an international staff and conducts business in English and French. The International Bureau of the court is available at all times to provide information and advice helpful to parties in resolving their disputes, even if the government of one or both of them is not a party to the Conventions of 1899 or 1907.

Pursuant to the rules on international commercial arbitration adopted by UNCITRAL in 1976, the secretary general of the PCA is empowered to designate an 'appointing authority' to break certain deadlocks that may arise in connection with the appointment and challenge of arbitrators in certain cases.

Administrative council
The administrative affairs of the PCA are supervised by the administrative council, which consists of the diplomatic representatives of the states parties to the Conventions accredited to the Netherlands. States continue to accede to the Convention of 1907, and are actively encouraged to do so, in order to strengthen the PCA and ensure that the largest possible number of states participate in determining its future course.

Arbitrators and commissioners, in the exercise of their duties outside their own countries, enjoy diplomatic privileges and immunities.

Procedural rules
The PCA continues to welcome new challenges in meeting the changing needs of the international community. Originally established to deal only with disputes between states, the PCA responded as early as 1935 to the need for dispute resolution in cases involving states and private parties. New Optional Rules, adopted in 1993 and 1994, provide a modern procedural framework for both types of arbitration. These rules are based closely on the UNCITRAL Arbitration Rules, thereby ensuring that they reflect modern arbitration practice and international consensus.

Optional rules
In 1992 the administrative council authorized the secretary general to establish rules of procedure to be known as the 'Permanent Court of Arbitration Optional Rules for Arbitrating Disputes between Two States', including model clauses on submission of disputes to arbitration. These rules of procedure were patterned after the UNCITRAL arbitration rules, with the assistance of a panel of experts convened by the secretary general.

Optional Rules for Arbitrating Disputes between Two Parties of which only One is a State were adopted in 1993.

Comment
As can be seen, it is both possible and desirable to set up an arbitral institution specifically tailored to deal with the unique problem of debt. The rationale behind ICSID can be adopted in setting up an international arbitration court. The debt crisis can be better resolved by institutions specifically committed to such problems. In other words, the proposed international arbitration court will be a specialized court in matters of debt.

Mode of establishing the court
It is desirable that the proposed international arbitration court be set up under the United Nations and by international treaty. Members of the United Nations in Article 3 of the UN Charter have agreed to 'settle their international disputes by peaceful means in such a manner that international peace and security, and justice are not endangered.'

Again, a General Assembly Resolution of 1970, after quoting Article 2 (3), of the UN Charter, proclaims: 'States shall accordingly seek early and just settlement of their international disputes by negotiation, inquiry, mediation, conciliation, arbitration, judicial settlement, resort to regional agencies or arrangements or other peaceful means of their choice.'

Establishing the court under the auspices of the UN would be the most logical step. In this regard, many Conventions relating to arbitration have been enacted under the auspices of the UN, including:

- Protocol on Arbitration Clauses, 1923
- Convention on the Execution of Foreign Arbitral Award, 1927
- Convention on the Recognition and Enforcement of Foreign Arbitral (New York), 1958
- UNCITRAL arbitration rules, 1976
- UNCITRAL conciliation rules, 1980
- UNCITRAL Model Law on International Arbitration, 1987
- UNCITRAL Notes on Organizing Arbitral Proceedings, 1996

The following preamble to the UNCITRAL arbitration rules embodied in Resolution 31/98 adopted by the General Assembly of the UN on 15 December 1976 is clear testimony that the UN really encourages arbitration as a method of settling disputes:

> The General Assembly,
> Recognizing the value of arbitration as a method of settling disputes arising in the context of international commercial relations,
> Being convinced that the establishment of rules for ad hoc arbitration that are acceptable in countries with different legal, social and economic systems would significantly contribute to the development of harmonious international economic relations,
> Bearing in mind that the Arbitration Rules of the United Nations Commission on International Trade Law have been prepared after extensive consultation with arbitral institutions and centres of international commercial arbitration,
> Noting that the Arbitration Rules were adopted by the United Nations Commission on International Trade Law at its ninth session after due deliberation,
> 1 Recommends the use of the Arbitration Rules of the United Nations Commission on International Trade Law in the settlement of disputes arising in the context of international commercial relations, particularly by reference to the Arbitration Rules in commercial contracts,
> 2 Requests the Secretary-General to arrange for the widest possible distribution of the Arbitration Rules.

Having recommended the establishment of the court by international treaty, it is essential to explain the meaning of a treaty and how it operates in international law. Treaties are a more direct and formal method of international law creation. States transact a vast amount of work by using the device of the treaty, in circumstances which underline the paucity of international law procedures when compared with the many ways in which a person within a state's internal border may set up binding rights and obligations. Wars will be terminated, disputes settled, territory acquired, special interests determined, alliances established and international organizations created all by means of treaties. No simpler method of reflecting the agreed objectives of states really exists and the international convention has to suffice both for straightforward bilateral agreements and complicated multilateral expressions of opinions. Thus, the concept of the treaty and how it operates becomes of paramount importance to the evolution of international law.

A treaty is basically an agreement between parties on the international scene. Although treaties may be concluded, or made, between states and international organizations, they are in essence concerned with relations between states. An International Convention on the Law of Treaties was signed in 1969 and came into force in 1980, while a Convention on Treaties between States and International Organizations was signed in 1986.

The 1969 Vienna Convention on the Law of Treaties partly reflects customary law and constitutes the basic framework for any discussion of the nature and characteristics of treaties. The fundamental principle of treaty law is undoubtedly the proposition that treaties are binding upon the parties to them and must be performed in good faith. This rule is known in legal terms as *pacta sunt servanda* and is arguably the oldest principle of international law. It was reaffirmed in Article 26 of the 1969 Convention, and underlies every international agreement. It is not hard to see why this is so. In the absence of a certain minimum belief that states will fulfil their treaty obligations in good faith, there is no reason for countries to enter into such obligations with each other.

The term 'treaty' itself is the one most used in the context of international agreements, but there are a variety of names which can be used to express the same concept, such as 'protocol', 'act', 'charter', 'covenant', 'pact' and 'concordat'. They each refer to the same basic activity and the use of one term rather than another often signifies little more than a desire for variety of expression.

A treaty is defined in Article 2 (for the purpose of the Convention) as 'an international agreement concluded between states in written form and governed by international law, whether embodied in a single instrument or in two or more related instruments and whatever its particular designation.' In other words, in addition to excluding agreements involving international organizations, the Convention does not cover agreements between states, which are to be governed by municipal law, such as a large number of commercial accords. This does not mean that such arrangements cannot be characterized as international agreements, or that they are invalid, merely because they are not within the purview of the 1969 Convention. Indeed, Article 3 stresses that international agreements between states and other subjects of international law or between two or more subjects of international law, or oral agreements, do not lose their validity by being excluded from the framework of the Convention. One important requirement is that the parties to the treaty intend to create legal relations as between themselves by means of their agreement. This is logical, since many agreements between states are merely statements of commonly held principles or objectives and are not intended to establish binding obligations.

There is no doubt that international commercial arbitration has gained worldwide acceptance as the normal means of resolving international commercial disputes and that international treaties on arbitration have been signed or adhered to with impressive success. A treaty establishing the proposed international arbitration court on debt would fit very well.

Structure of the court

As for the terms of reference for establishing such a court, there is no harm in the court being composed of not more than five arbitrators from both the debtor and creditor sides, with an independent arbitrator to ensure impartiality. This kind of composition has been used in other arbitral tribunals, referred to above. It is universally accepted that a tribunal should be composed of an uneven number of arbitrators, to make it possible for decisions to be reached. However, such a court can also maintain a panel of arbitrators from which parties can choose.

Like any other arbitral institution, the proposed court should have a secretariat to provide necessary organizational support. Facilities such as courtrooms, a library, consultation rooms, etc., should also be provided. Support staff should be employed to provide technical support to arbitrators and parties, as well as organize hearings and provide administrative support.

Jurisdiction, procedure, parties, rules and sources of law

There are a lot of arbitration rules in existence, which can be adopted for use by the court with regard to procedural matters. UNCITRAL Arbitration Rules, for example, have been widely adopted by arbitral institutions worldwide. These rules regulate the procedure that may be used in arbitral proceedings. Parties to arbitral proceedings are also at liberty to agree on the rules to apply to the arbitration. Arbitration depends a lot on the agreement or consent of parties.

The proposed international arbitration court may also make its own rules for the conduct of proceedings. Some arbitral institutions already formulate their own rules for use in proceedings. Like UNCITRAL rules, such rules may cover a variety of aspects, including the mode of instituting proceedings, how to make applications before the court, time limits, filing of documents, mode of hearing matters, etc.

Above all, the main instrument for constituting the court, defining its functions, and structuring and prescribing its jurisdiction, would be the enabling international treaty. The international treaty should be the primary source of law to define the jurisdiction and types of matters that may be adjudicated upon, the kinds of loans covered (e.g. government loans or private loans guaranteed by the government), and the parties who may institute legal proceedings. The treaty may be supplemented by rules of procedure adopted or made by the court. Parties should, however, remain free to decide on the type of law to apply to the dispute. International law will also generally apply to the proceedings.

The treaty is the only document that can make it possible for debtors to obtain relief from the debt burden. Thus the treaty should be signed and ratified by as many creditors as possible, especially those in the Paris Club. The treaty will only bind those creditors who sign the treaty. This is why it is important to have such a treaty enacted under the auspices of the United Nations.

The treaty should be prepared in such a way that it takes care of the interests of both creditors and debtors. The treaty will inevitably also recognize the importance of giving effect to loan agreements made between creditors and debtors. It will also address issues of enforcement of such agreements, as well as recovery of doubtful or dubious debts, the writing off of some debts, rescheduling, etc. The treaty and the rules should also give latitude to parties to negotiate or employ mediation or conciliation in the settlement of disputes.

The treaty and the rules may also provide for arbitration proceedings to be instituted by states, NGOs or even individuals. The idea of allowing states and individuals to file claims or actions is justified from the human rights point of view. The government of a country and its peoples should be able to seek redress in this type of court. After all, issues of debt directly affect the people of a country. Thus, persons with a legitimate interest should have a right to institute proceedings in this court. As an example, the African Charter on Human and People's Rights promulgated by the Organization of African Unity (the predecessor to the African Union) provided for an African Commission to monitor the implementation of the Charter. The commission was made up of 11 members nominated by states parties to the Charter and then elected by the entire OAU Assembly. The commission had *inter alia* the following main areas of responsibility:

1. Ensuring the protection of the rights and duties covered under the African Charter.
2. Examining complaints made by one state party against another.
3. Examining complaints submitted by individuals and NGOs against states which have ratified the Charter.

Thus there is no harm in allowing states, NGOs and individuals to file actions.

The treaty and the court rules should also address issues of legal costs for such proceedings, especially where individuals are concerned. Such costs should be borne by states parties to the treaty who are finally adjudged to be at fault. Some individuals (especially from poor countries) may not be able to afford legal fees. Hence, there must be provision for Legal Aid or financial assistance from a fund created by states parties to the treaty.

To save costs, the court should also be at liberty to sit at venues convenient to parties to litigation. However, parties should also be given the latitude to decide on the venue, as is usual in arbitration.

As in any other type of arbitral proceedings, the parties to an action should be heard and should be given the chance to adduce evidence and advance arguments concerning non-payment or unpayable dubious or illegitimate loans. Parties (creditors or debtors) could be represented by advocates, attorneys or lay representatives of their choice. Arbitrators would decide (render an award) if parties fail to reach agreement. The award should depend on evidence adduced, the agreement between the parties and rules of equity and fairness, as well as international law. The court should be required to hear all the parties before it and should be informal in its procedure and should not adhere to legal technicalities like in the traditional court system.

The court would also be required to examine technical details and information relating to accounts, economics, budgets, availability of resources and impact of the debt on the nation, and reach decisions that also take into account the concerns and interests of the creditor country. The court should not assume the character of a lopsided and biased institution meant only to serve the interests of debtors, as it will lose legitimacy, credibility and respect. It should be impartial and fair, and resolve disputes according to the rule of law and respect for human rights.

Stay of proceedings

It is a common feature of court and arbitral proceedings for parties to apply for a stay of proceedings pending disposal of arbitral proceedings. Under this power, repayment of a particular disputed loan may be frozen, stayed or suspended until the court makes a decision. This power may be vested in the court by treaty and the rules of the court. The idea is to maintain the status quo until an action is disposed of.

Remedies and enforcement of an award

The court as an arbitral institution should be able to make decisions according to internationally accepted norms of justice, taking into account the interests of the parties and the agreement between the parties. Where appropriate, the decision or award may include debt rescheduling or cancellation in cases of illegitimate, dubious debt. The court may also award compensation (reparations), depending on the facts of each particular case. However, these issues, which are related to jurisdiction and the functions of the court, should be specifically vested by the enabling treaty. State parties must agree by treaty to give such powers to this court.

The enforcement of any award or decision of the court should be done in accordance with the enabling treaty or existing treaties on the enforcement of arbitral awards. In particular, enforcement mechanisms and powers available under ICSID, constituted under the ICSID Convention, may be adopted and embodied in the treaty. Articles 53–5 of the said Convention (on recognition and enforcement of awards) provide as follows:

> Article 53
> The award shall be binding on the parties and shall not be subject to any appeal or to any other remedy except those provided for in this Convention. Each party shall abide by and comply with the terms of the award except to the extent that enforcement shall have been stayed pursuant to the relevant provisions of this Convention.
> For the purposes of this Section, 'award' shall include any decision interpreting, revising or annulling such award pursuant to Articles 50, 51 or 52.
>
> Article 54
> Each Contracting State shall recognize an award rendered pursuant to this Convention as binding and enforce the pecuniary obligations imposed by that award within its territories as if it were a final judgement of a court in that State. A Contracting State with a federal constitution may enforce such an award in or through its federal courts and may provide that such courts shall treat the award as if it were a final judgement of the courts of a constituent state.
> A party seeking recognition or enforcement in the territories of a Contracting State shall furnish to a competent court or other authority, which such State shall have designated for this purpose, a copy of the award certified by the Secretary-General. Each Contracting State shall notify the Secretary-General of the designation of the competent court or other authority for this purpose and of any subsequent change in such designation.
> Execution of the award shall be governed by the laws concerning the execution of judgements in force in the State in whose territories such execution is sought.
>
> Article 55
> Nothing in Article 54 shall be construed as derogating from the law in force in any Contracting State relating to immunity of that State or of any foreign State from execution.

Implication of the Proposed Arbitration Mechanism

At present, there is no alternative dispute settlement mechanism that addresses the complex issues of debt. All the existing arbitral institutions may only resolve disputes according to the agreement between parties and rules relating to international commercial arbitration. An institution created by treaty can be endowed with special powers to deal with any new situation.

This kind of institution would continue to be neutral depending on the calibre of arbitrators, their skills and their backgrounds. The treaty should provide for appointment of arbitrators who are impartial and professionally competent. The parties should also have a say in the type of arbitrators appointed. If there is any doubt as to the impartiality of any arbitrator, the parties should challenge the appointment and there must be provision in the treaty and the court rules for such a challenge against an arbitrator. Arbitrators who are properly trained and have judicial capacity will only decide cases according to the law and accepted norms of justice. They will not be swayed by the financial standing of parties.

Since international arbitration thrives on the will and consent of parties, which may be enshrined in the treaty, there is no reason why development cooperation between North and South should be effected. This is particularly so if a fair treaty is put in place through a forum like the United Nations. However, if the treaty is ratified only by a few states, then there will certainly be apprehension in the lending market. Naturally, lenders or creditors who prefer to dictate terms will view the treaty and powers of the court suspiciously and may want to operate outside the treaty. This may have a negative impact on the flow of capital and resources to less developed countries.

Since arbitration, mediation and conciliation depend on the consent of parties, the position of CSOs and third parties needs to be properly defined in the enabling treaty. The role of third parties in this context needs to be properly debated during the treaty-making process.

Creditors lend money to poor countries on terms that ensure some returns to the creditors. Creditors have their own business interests to protect as well. Thus, any over-politicization of what may be considered as commercial debts may alienate creditors from those who badly need resources (debtors). Confidence may be instilled by the setting up of credible institutions for the settlement of disputes, which are acceptable to all. This is how institutions like ICSID and the PCA have come to be accepted. In other words, it is important that states have confidence in the institutions they are going to use. Certainly, member states of the United Nations cannot have confidence in biased institutions which deliver purely political judgements. There must be respect for the rule of law and norms of justice.

Once states parties to the treaty gain confidence in the performance of the court, they will respect its decisions, whether or not they win or lose. Again, the states which sign and ratify the treaty will commit themselves to accepting as final and binding the decisions or awards rendered by the court. This is the practice adopted in respect of other international treaties. States parties to treaties must bind themselves to respect the provisions of the treaty and the institutions created under it. To give an example, members of the United Nations have bound themselves to accept the decisions of the International Court of Justice (ICJ) as binding and final. Under Article 60 of the Statute of the ICJ, decisions or judgements of the court are final and not subject to appeal. By virtue of Article 2, the ICJ is composed of 15 members:

> Elected regardless of their nationality, from among persons of high moral character, who possess the qualifications required in their respective countries for appointment to the highest judicial offices, or are jurisconsults of recognized competence in international law.

The appointment of competent jurists to sit either as judges or arbitrators can instil confidence in the parties.

Of course, if the suggested arbitration mechanisms are undermined or inoperative and creditors believe that the money they lend is insecure, they will withdraw lending facilities or even apply sanctions to force debtors to pay. Since creditors operate in cartels, they can easily do this. If they are suspicious of the suggested mechanisms, then debt cancellation, rescheduling and fair treatment of debtors will remain a pipe dream.

The United Nations depends on the will and consent of state parties to its Charter. Thus, if a treaty introducing an international arbitration court on debt is enacted under the UN, the role of the UN as a key player in the amicable settlement of disputes and democratic global governance will be enhanced. Such a treaty will be an addition to the many conventions that have been enacted in the area of arbitration. Arbitration is not a new concept to the United Nations.

The establishment of a unique and specialized court in issues of debt will ensure that such problems are given due attention and are addressed fairly in a professional, technical manner. There will also be proper understanding of the problem. The issue of debt can only be dealt with properly by experts through an orderly process and specialized forum. The issue is so serious that there must be concerted efforts to solve it.

Recovery of Money Stolen by Leaders and Put in Foreign Banks

Arbitration thrives on the consent and agreement of parties. Again, rules of natural justice apply which entail the hearing of parties to arbitral proceedings. Thus, an arbitral decision or award which excludes parties from a hearing, or is deliberately made in the absence of a party, is a nullity. According to accepted norms of justice, an order can only be made against a person if they are a party to the proceedings and have been heard. Parties who are affected by proceedings should be joined to these legal proceedings and should be afforded an opportunity to present their cases or defend themselves (either in person or through their legal representatives).

To make an order against a politician or leader alleged to have stolen money, the arbitral institution must conduct a trial and even hear the person concerned. Problems may arise if they cannot be found. Thus, it is better to leave such problems to the criminal law courts. It is submitted that there are adequate criminal laws for the arrest and recovery of property of fugitive political leaders. Stealing money and depositing it in a foreign bank is a serious criminal offence (felony), which is also subject to extradition laws. States should be encouraged to enter into extradition treaties with each other. Such treaties should include provisions for recovering property feloniously obtained, so that it can be returned to the countries from where it was stolen. This position is accepted internationally. The

United Nations in fact encourages states to enter into extradition treaties as a way of fighting crime.

Parties must be encouraged to utilize existing criminal laws rather than resort to arbitration, which is a civil process and thus not ideal for such a purpose. The ultimate recovery of stolen money should depend on the application of criminal laws relating to money laundering, theft, fraud and unlawful externalization, etc. Organizations like the International Police (Interpol) can be strengthened for this purpose.

Conclusion

The establishment of an international criminal court on debt is long overdue. The problem of debt requires innovative solutions. Existing mechanisms do not adequately address the problem of debt. The court should be used strictly for the settlement of civil disputes and not for the enforcement of criminal laws.

3

Sovereign Debt Restructuring Mechanism

Jubilee USA Network

When it becomes necessary for a state to declare itself bankrupt, in the same manner as when it becomes necessary for an individual to do so, a fair, open and avowed bankruptcy is always the measure which is both least dishonourable to the debtor, and least hurtful to the creditor. (Adam Smith, 1776)

INTRODUCTION

After a decade of national debt insolvency, debt campaigners around the world have been calling for the establishment of an international bankruptcy procedure for countries.

Never before have the world's wealthiest countries with a preponderant voice in the international financial system so seriously appreciated the need for a more efficient, expeditious and orderly procedure for dealing with bankruptcies of entire nations. The recurrent financial crises have necessitated a political response to the concern about the possibility of future crises. The existing procedures and large taxpayer-funded 'bailouts' used to handle them have been too ad hoc and have not addressed the underlying problems associated with national debt burdens.

Anne Krueger, the International Monetary Fund's first deputy managing director, has become the most influential and articulate proponent of its proposed answer: the Sovereign Debt Restructuring Mechanism (SDRM). The IMF unveiled the proposal for discussion in 2002. In the 1990s the creditor community had become 'increasingly diverse and diffuse' because private creditors offer more financing to some (middle-income) developing countries than do governments through traditional foreign aid. Because of this, the IMF has acknowledged that there is a need for a new international legal framework for sovereign debtors, designed to replicate the useful features of domestic bankruptcy proceedings.

Such a mechanism could be enacted with an amendment to the IMF's Articles of Agreement, if its major shareholders, the Group of Seven governments (G7), were willing to do so. The IMF's proposed mechanism would allow a qualified majority of creditors to approve a restructuring agreement for countries and make that decision binding on the remaining minority of creditors. The restructuring procedure would be triggered by request of the debtor nation and be subject to agreement of the IMF or some proportion of creditors. It would, suggests Ms Krueger, be invoked only to deal with a debt burden that is 'clearly unsustainable', not with temporary debt crises (illiquidity).

Michael Gavin, of the private creditor UBS Warburg, offered a more frank assessment of why the international financial institutions (IFIs) may finally be addressing the problem:

> The problem isn't so much that the existing system poses insuperable barriers to debt restructuring. While there's room for improvement, experience suggests that it doesn't. The problem for them is that, when they want to cut-off a country with debt problems, they have no answer to the question 'what are we supposed to do now'? These process-minded people need a 'process', a 'road-map', or they will feel like they're pushing the borrowing government into a procedural 'black hole'. They want to fill up the 'black hole' with answers to the question 'what next' so that they can cut-off countries earlier, before they become a potentially worrisome charge on their taxpayer's balance sheet. You may or may not like this motivation, but it's a political imperative for most industrial-country governments right now.' (Global Emerging Markets Daily, 17 March 2003)

Both the proposed SDRM and the current Heavily-Indebted Poor Country (HIPC) initiative are efforts by the IMF and World Bank to respond to the growing international public pressure placed on government officials to do something about the unacceptable and deepening debt crisis.

What is the SDRM Proposal?

SDRM is a system that would allow a national government to request the convening of a disinterested international panel that would negotiate with a government's private creditors and arrive at a debt restructuring agreement that requires approval by a majority of the creditors that would then be enforceable on all of the country's private creditors. This would be a new development because under existing procedures, any single private creditor can refuse to accept a restructuring arrangement and instead attempt to sue a national government for full payment of debts under the original repayment terms.

SDRM would not allow for a stay or standstill on debt payments while a restructuring agreement is arranged, as a domestic bankruptcy proceeding does. Nor would it include any public debts owed to governments or multilateral lending institutions such as the World Bank and IMF. Therefore, only the wealthiest middle-income countries that hold mostly private sector debt would stand to benefit from SDRM, whereas many more of the poorer countries that mostly owe public debt would not have their needs addressed.

What would it mean for indebted countries?

As with bankruptcy procedures for individual persons or companies, the proposed SDRM would provide nations with a procedure to restructure the terms of repayment of debts to their private creditors along lines more favourable to nations. However, SDRM would provide only a reprieve for countries, not a final solution to the debt crisis. The SDRM proposal would not cancel a country's debts, but would instead make the repayment of the debts more manageable. Additionally, the IMF would only approve the debt restructuring if the indebted country first satisfactorily implements a host of economic policy reforms deemed necessary by the IMF. Such reforms, known as structural adjustment programmes (SAPs), include trade and financial liberalization, severe budget austerity, privatization of public enterprises, and other radical reforms that have been highly controversial for over twenty years and have failed to increase per capita economic growth rates or reduce poverty rates in developing countries.

RESPONSES TO THE SDRM PROPOSAL

Group of Seven

There has been a lot of discussion of SDRM over the past year and the IMF has continued to reformulate various features of the mechanism in accordance with the feedback it has received. The G7 finance ministers and central bank governors called for a finalized proposal by the time of the spring 2003 IMF/World Bank meetings. The G7 has not yet formally endorsed the SDRM approach and is still considering an alternative proposal favoured by the United States.

US Treasury

The US prefers an alternative proposal that deals with the national debt insolvency problem through the writing of new collective action clauses (CACs) into the bonds issued by governments. Such clauses would compel all bond holders to be party to any debt restructuring arrangements in the future, should it be deemed necessary, and would prevent any bond holders from refusing to participate in a restructuring, as current practice allows. This would mean that all bond holders would have to cooperate and share any setbacks in losses or extended repayment that result from a restructuring. Because such CACs have not been included in previous bond issues, private creditors were unwilling to enter into restructuring proceedings for fear that some would take deeper losses than others.

John B. Taylor, Under Secretary of Treasury for International Affairs, has stated that the US will fully consider its decentralized CACs approach, the IMF's centralized SDRM approach, or a combination of the two, and attempt to determine which it thinks will work best. Taylor explained some of the key differences between the clause approach and SDRM:

- SDRM would aggregate claims across different types of bond issues and debts, while the clause approach would not.
- SDRM would establish a panel or court, while the clause approach would not.
- SDRM would override existing bond contracts, while the clauses would apply only to new issues, or perhaps to old issues if they are swapped for new issues.
- The clause approach could be implemented quickly, while SDRM would require a good deal of time in light of its relative complexity and the need to gain legislative approval, including in the United States.

The IMF's response to the US clause approach is that when there are hundreds of debt contracts governed by the laws of many jurisdictions, CACs in individual contracts would fail to ensure coordination among creditors. In contrast, the proposed SDRM would force private creditors to cooperate.

Private creditors

Private creditors are very opposed to the proposed SDRM because it would institutionalize a process that they fear may make it too easy for governments to default, and that this may inspire governments to do so more frequently. Private creditors are concerned that such a formal process would generally undermine the sanctity of contracts between creditors and debtors, something that they believe is the basis for all financial activity. The SDRM proposal is also unpopular among private creditors because it excludes official, or public, debts (those provided by governments bilaterally or in multilateral lending institutions) from the process, and leaves only private creditors to take a financial loss in any restructuring process.

These concerns over the proposed SDRM have been registered, for example, in the Trade Association of the Emerging Markets (EMTA) position paper: 'The possibility of an overriding bankruptcy regime chills the market-based approach because neither creditors nor issuers know what changes can safely be made in existing documentation.'

Governments in the global South

The governments of many indebted developing countries in the global South share a concern with private creditors about the impact of the proposed SDRM: that lending would become riskier and result in few loans being made to developing countries, a development which might actually make insolvency crises more frequent. Another concern is that a country claiming debt insolvency might face a loss of access to capital markets. In turn, if private capital markets become less willing to lend, it would increase the foreign aid burden on the rich countries and reverse the general trend of the 1990s, in which private creditors increasingly replaced traditional bilateral or multilateral foreign aid to middle-income developing countries.

Non-governmental organizations and civil society groups in the South

Most NGOs and civil society groups in the developing countries, including the various Jubilee South groups and other debt-cancellation advocacy groups, have expressed vociferous opposition to the IMF's proposed SDRM. This opposition is well articulated by Demba Dembele of the Forum for African Alternatives in Dakar, Senegal and the international Jubilee South coalition:

> It's one more way for the IMF to control the fate of indebted governments. The institution that already makes loans and decides which countries are creditworthy would also be in charge of managing the appeals process and designing new economic austerity programmes that will continue to starve the poor to feed the rich.

Jubilee USA Network Rejects IMF's SDRM Proposal

The Jubilee USA Network welcomes the IMF's admission that the crisis of unsustainable debt burdens in developing countries has not been resolved. However, it shares the concerns of many of our Jubilee South partners that the IMF's proposed

SDRM is both inadequate and potentially harmful to the people of indebted nations.

The Jubilee USA Network criticizes the SDRM proposal for the following reasons:

- SDRM applies only to debts claimed by the private sector. To be fair, the IMF and World Bank must also put their share of the debt portfolio on the table.
- SDRM puts the IMF at the centre of the process: it would convene the 'independent' panel, determine whether a country legitimately needs the assistance provided by the mechanism, and help design and monitor the policies that debtor countries would commit to at the time of restructuring.
- A 'standstill' provision that would have allowed governments to suspend debt payments without the threat of legal action during the time that the restructuring is negotiated has been removed from the latest version of the SDRM proposal.

The Jubilee USA Network believes the primary issue that must be addressed is the failure of the HIPC initiative adequately to resolve the crisis of the crushing debt burden in so many of the world's poorest countries. Attention focused on the SDRM proposal may simply sweep the failure of HIPC under the rug to avoid the seriousness of the continuing debt crisis.

In contrast to SDRM, the Jubilee USA Network believes that any mechanism to address debt must be a much more fair and transparent international arbitration process that could apply to all indebted countries, not just those the IMF deems insolvent. Such an arbitration process would have citizen participation and government accountability at the centre of any decisions about the fate of public debt restructuring in their countries.

The Jubilee USA Network also believes another important issue that must be addressed is the illegitimacy of much of the existing debts - the decades of loans to dictators which were stolen with the knowledge and even collusion of creditors; the loans used as tools for suppressing democracy; the loans for failures such as wasteful and harmful development projects. The SDRM proposal does not provide for the acknowledgement of illegitimate debts.

The IMF shapes the outcome

The proposed SDRM would ensure that the IMF would play a pre-emptive role in shaping the outcome of any debt crisis resolution negotiations by setting the country's level of 'debt sustainability' from which the necessary debt reduction would logically follow. In addition, under the proposed SDRM, the IMF would continue its existing role of determining the debtor's economic policies. As a result, the IMF would effectively draft the 'composition plan' that should rightly be presented by the debtor, and that would provide the basis for negotiations between the debtor and creditors. By filing the 'plan', the IMF effectively disempowers the debtor, all other creditors and civil society. The IMF would probably set 'debt sustainability' at a level that does not place its own claims economically at risk, even if they were legally exempt from debt cancellation. All of these features of the proposed SDRM would allow the IMF to play the role of judge in its own cause - the defence of its own claims - which would amount to an unacceptable conflict of interest. The IMF is not an impartial actor in these decisions and should not be afforded so much control over any such sovereign debt restructuring mechanism.

Of course, the IMF does this already. However, by enshrining SDRM in its Articles of Agreement, the Fund would be strengthened in this role. It would increase its importance by obtaining the sole mandate for debt restructuring. (An amendment to its Articles would elevate the role of the IMF above that of the World Bank, and would change the present situation in which the IMF and the Bank together engage in poor country debt management.) The amendment to the Articles would legalize the practice of ensuring the IMF as 'preferred creditor', which means its debt will be serviced before any other creditors (until now the IFIs enjoyed de facto but not de jure preferred creditor status). In other words, amending the Articles to incorporate the proposed SDRM would legalize and strengthen the IMF's current practice.

How SDRM Compares to HIPC

The recent attention given to the IMF's proposed SDRM has overshadowed the much broader problem of heavily indebted poor countries that may not be at the point of bankruptcy, yet which still pay hundreds of millions of dollars in debts, undermining efforts to reduce poverty and fight HIV/AIDS. The heavy debt burden of impoverished countries was supposed to be dealt with by the current HIPC debt relief initiative. Both the SDRM proposal and HIPC deal with the problem of countries in deep debt crises, but they are very different structures. The SDRM proposal does not fix the problems of the current HIPC, and the inadequacy of the current level of debt relief on offer in the HIPC continues to have a very negative impact on many of the world's poorest countries.

Similarities between HIPC and SRDM

- Both the proposed SDRM and the current HIPC initiative are efforts by the IMF and World Bank to respond to the growing international public pressure placed on government officials to do something about the deepening debt crisis.
- Both programmes fall far short of adequately addressing the real problems at issue by doing nothing to solve the debt crisis. (Both programmes are designed to keep countries from defaulting on their debts to creditors, but to not get them out of debt entirely).
- Both programmes include the continuation of the highly controversial structural adjustment programs that have failed to achieve higher economic growth rates or reduce poverty over the last 20 years.
- Both programmes are designed and operated by the politically powerful countries of the G7 who exercise the bulk of control over the decision-making processes at the IMF.

Differences between HIPC and SRDM

- SDRM would primarily involve only 15-20 of the wealthier emerging market economies, such as Mexico, Venezuela or Argentina and other middle-income countries. In contrast, the HIPC initiative only deals with the 42 most heavily indebted poor countries, most of them extremely poor and are categorized as low-income or least-developed countries (LDCs).
- SDRM only would enable countries to restructure the debts to their private creditors. It does not include 'public' or 'official' debts held by bilateral governments or multilateral lending agencies such as the IMF and World Bank. This contrasts sharply with HIPC, which deals with very poor countries whose debts largely comprise public debt and include very little, if any, private creditor debt. Because the SDRM proposal would only restructure debts held by private creditors, even relatively generous reductions by the private sector might be insufficient for a country to get a fresh start if bilateral and multilateral debts are not also included and reduced in the debt restructuring process.

The proposed SDRM will not fix the problems with HIPC

Several problems with the current HIPC initiative are in desperate need of legislative and other corrections, and none of these continuing problems with HIPC are addressed by the IMF's SDRM.

- Not only were the future economic growth projections of HIPC countries over-optimistic and the debt sustainability threshold of 150 per cent debt-to-exports too high, but also commodity prices for major exports from the HIPC countries have fallen on world markets. This has lowered economic growth rates even further, and plunged many HIPCs deeper into debt unsustainability.
- Given the current official debt sustainability threshold, the HIPC countries still do not have enough revenues left over to effectively achieve the Millennium Development Goals by 2015.
- The HIPC initiative continues to be contingent upon countries implementing the highly controversial structural adjustment economic policy reforms that have largely failed either to reduce poverty or achieve high rates of economic growth for over twenty years. Further, the Poverty Reduction Strategy Papers process circumvents NGOs and civil society groups and prevents them proposing alternative policy choices in their national PRSPs.
- Countries continue to fail to comply with IMF structural adjustment conditions, and have continuously fallen 'off-track' in the HIPC process.
- Some non-participating creditors have brought lawsuits against HIPCs to prevent the cancellation of their debts.
- Additional 'Topping Up' financing from bilaterals should not be used until the structure of HIPC is fixed.
- Not enough heavily indebted poor countries are included in the 42 HIPC countries; there are several other countries that are also in desperate need of debt cancellation.

Table 1:
Similarities and differences among the existing HIPC initiative, the IMF's proposed SRDM, and what Jubilee USA Network would prefer to see in a fair and transparent arbitration process.

	HIPC	SDRM	FTAP
Which countries are eligible?	up to 42 of the most heavily indebted poor countries holding mostly public debt	15-20 wealthier emerging market economies holding mostly private debt	all developing countries with external debts
What kind of debt is involved?	public debt owed to bilateral and multilateral creditors	private debt owed to private creditors	debt owed to both public and private creditors
Is the illegitimacy of debt considered?	no	no	yes
Who controls the programme?	IMF, World Bank and the G7 governments	IMF, World Bank and the G7 governments	Global civil society organizations and creditors
Is implementing structural adjustment programmes a condition?	yes	yes	no
Function	partial debt cancellation	debt restructuring	100% debt cancellation or the appropriate levels of debt relief
Outcomes	will reduce countries' debt payments but will not get countries completely out of debt	will prevent countries from defaulting on foreign debts but will not get countries completely out of debt	will get most countries completely out of debt
Purpose	a response to public pressure to adddress debt crisis	a response to public pressure to address debt crisis	a process definitely to address the debt crisis

The IMF's SDRM proposal does nothing to address these problems with HIPC. To fully address the debt crisis, HIPCs would need full debt cancellation. There is a current legislative effort that seeks to have the HIPCs pay only 5 per cent of revenues in debt servicing, and 10 per cent for certain countries not experiencing severe health emergencies such as HIV/AIDS. There is still an urgent need to support current legislative proposals (such as the 5-10 per cent approach) that seek to improve upon the HIPC initiative.

A Fair and Transparent Arbitration Process

If an international debt insolvency mechanism is to be established, the Jubilee USA Network believes it must be a much more fair and transparent international arbitration process (FTAP) that could apply to all indebted countries, not just those the IMF deems insolvent. The very existence of such a framework, enabling any indebted nation to file for a standstill on debt payments, or for its creditors to declare the country insolvent, would amount to a form of regulation of international capital flow and would discipline both lax lenders and reckless borrowers. Such an FTAP would allow illegitimate debts to be assessed and annulled and would likely free countries of the bulk of the current debt burdens.

The criteria for petitioning for a standstill on payments would be determined by the debtor nation, not the IMF or any other creditors. For the Jubilee movement, debts that can only be repaid at a cost to the fundamental human rights of the population are deemed unpayable debts. An FTAP would remove international creditors, like the IMF, from playing the role of plaintiff, judge and jury in the event of international debt crises. Central to the framework of an FTAP would be the independence of the insolvency court. The court would be an ad hoc body, appointed to deal with each individual petition for insolvency. It would not require an international treaty.

Under an FTAP, the IMF would not be able to influence the appointment or the proceedings of the ad hoc independent panel. The sovereign debtor on the one hand, and creditors on the other, would determine the composition of the court. Both sides would nominate one representative each; the two representatives would then choose a third, in whom they both have confidence, to act as the judge. The proceedings of an FTAP court would be completely transparent and accountable to creditors, but most importantly, to the citizens of debtor nations. The court will assess all debts and ascertain if they were contracted legitimately.

Because an FTAP would deal with resolving crises involving public money, public participation in the process would be key. Such public involvement would facilitate the accountability to the electorate of government officials responsible for reckless borrowing in debtor nations and would underscore the liabilities for lax and corrupt lending in creditor nations. Both of these features would introduce discipline into the future lending and borrowing processes, and challenge corruption.

4
Guayaquil Declaration on New Financial Architecture

Jubilee 2000 Red Guayaquil

From 9-12 March 2001in Guayaquil, Ecuador, delegations from around the world met to consider alternatives to the current deeply biased unilateral mechanism for the restructuring and management of sovereign debt. They agreed the following:

- The current system of debt restructuring and management, before and during debt crises, in which international creditors play the role of plaintiff, prosecutor, judge and jury, is unjust and designed to protect the interests of creditors, with total disregard for the fundamental human rights of the people of debtor countries.
- The current system – which gives a principal role to creditor organizations such as the Paris Club, the London Club and the International Monetary Fund (IMF) – must be replaced by a new financial architecture.
- Current financial architecture shifts the whole burden of debt to the debtor nation and its people, and protects international creditors from co-responsibility, risk, liability and loss.
- The IMF's proposal for a Sovereign Debt Restructuring Mechanism (SDRM) is deeply flawed: (a) it does not alter the balance of power between sovereign debtor and international creditors; (b) it maintains effective creditor control of debtor nations, through the IMF; (c) it is a non-transparent and unaccountable mechanism; (d) it does not include Heavily Indebted Poor Countries (HIPC) debtor nations; (e) it exempts the IMF and World Bank loans from debt write-off.

The new financial architecture that we propose borrows from internationally accepted legal principles of insolvency, and seeks to transform the current architecture and to provide a just solution to the problem of sovereign debt restructuring and management, based on the following principles:

- The establishment of an independent tribunal for debt justice.
- An open, transparent and accountable process for this independent tribunal. The setting up of public audits of the sovereign debt, and of hearings related to the debt, is an integral part of the tribunal's deliberations.
- The subordination of creditor interests to the fundamental human rights of people in debtor nations, as enshrined in international UN charters and declarations.
- The recognition that sovereign debt is public debt, and therefore that citizens have a right to participate and influence the arbitral tribunal, and be central to the outcome of its award.
- The right of the debtor nation to declare a standstill on debt payments when further debt servicing is likely to violate fundamental human rights.
- The co-responsibility of creditors and the debtor governments for illegit-

imately contracted debts and the power of the tribunal to dismiss those claims.

- The recognition that this new architecture is not merely a technical or bureaucratic alternative, but a fundamentally political transformation in the existing unjust balance of power between international finance and debtor nations and their people.
- In place of creditor-determined conditionalities, there should be a new framework in which a debtor government commits itself to defend human rights, through (among other things) social and infrastructure investment, and further commits itself to openness, accountability and democratization of financial management.
- Civil society organizations must begin a mobilization aimed at popularizing a fair and transparent arbitral debt tribunal and putting it firmly on the international agenda for change.

INTRODUCTION TO ARBITRATION
Arbitration's objectives are the following:

- Provide a new opportunity to finance development.
- Automatic moratorium and protection to confront creditors.
- IMF to initiate the process and provide access to capital during times of insolvency.
- Participation from civil society within debtor countries.

A fair arbitration mechanism would maintain the distinction between legal debt and illegal debt.

Anne Krueger of the IMF recognizes the problems of the international monetary and financial system and has suggested the possibility of halting the payment of external debts under certain circumstances, with the support of the IMF. However, reforms and adjustment have not solved the problem of external debt; instead, they have generated permanent crisis and instability. The IMF's policies have not been successful in Latin America, for example, as demonstrated by the Argentinean crisis. This has deligitimated the IMF and nothing can be done to religitimate it. The fight against the IMF requires coordination between the North and South, which hitherto has not been strong. Wider campaigns and academic discussions on arbitration within the United Nations are also essential.

Arbitration as a process should result in better development within debtor countries. The process is initiated if a state declares its foreign debt unpayable because its social development is being damaged. This implies an automatic debt standstill.

Clearly, arbitration must take into account the implementation of human rights (economic and social). It should not be necessary to wait for crisis and the unpayability of debt in order to commence an arbitration process. It is for debtor countries to determine whether they need to seek arbitration. There is an ethical dimension to the issue, which centres on the relative importance of various actors in the arbitration process.

- The basis for international arbitration is to be found to a large extent in international treaties on human rights, which give priority to the meeting of basic human needs such as health and education.
- Any country can submit its external debt to an arbitration framework, for a resolution of the crisis, with the following justifications: a) The unpayability of the scheduled debt service; b) The illegitimacy of the debt, due to corruption or fraud, 'odious' debt, or any other form of illegitimacy.
- There must be pressure from civil society to make governments take a proactive role in the process, to prevent the collapse of a country's economy and because of debt illegitimacy.
- Civil society must create instruments, establish standards and set indicators to monitor external debt in each country, to determine whether it is justified in applying for arbitration.

The Functioning of an Independent Arbitration Framework

The issue of a framework is based on two elements: (1) an ad hoc procedure or (2) appeal to an institution (international court). The debate focuses on various criteria:

- The risk of arbitration being a slow and insecure process, subject to interruption. It also implies the legitimization of debt.
- Initiating an arbitration process should also be seen as part of a strategy to change international structural relationships.
- An ad hoc procedure could be implemented first and institutionalized afterwards.
- Any institutionalization assumes that the United States would be willing to submit itself.
- There exists the possibility of using existing institutions in the field of human rights (e.g. the UN Declaration of Human Rights, the Inter-American Court).
- Any solution needs to tackle a set of problems; there are no individual solutions.

Arbitration will not completely solve the problem of debt or underdevelopment, but it nevertheless constitutes a viable framework. The economic and ethical unpayability of debt should be a moral umbrella, which does not impede the elaboration and forwarding of other proposals, such as an international treaty, which allows the use of legal instruments in existing human rights institutions, supported by a mobilized civil society.

The institutionalization of an ad hoc procedure implies a very long process involving changes in juridical structures, the establishment of an international court and an increase in bureaucracy, which could lead to greater manipulation by those countries that hold political and economical power.

Conditionalities and Applications

The real debate is about the conditions of an arbitration process (for example, the social control of liberated funds). This is also important for creditors when it refers to matters of corruption and democratization – as when former debt-country negotiators afterwards become the employees of multilaterals.

It is important that governments assume responsibility for including in future budgets all the funds needed to guarantee people's basic rights and needs, and that they accept the participation of civil society in discussion and control – as in the Bolivian experience of social participation in devising anti-poverty programmes, and in the control liberated funds through HIPICH and external funds in general.

'Conditionality' is associated with the IMF's proposals: we should perhaps talk about positive conditions, using the word 'framework'.

Opportunities and Requirements for Real Participation of Civil Society in Arbitration Processes

The participation of civil society in arbitration processes is decisive because governments do not represent the interests of the majority of citizens and have compromised with international financial capital, which deepens their lack of representation. However, civil society is not homogeneous. In addition, governments, the IMF, World Bank and other international financial institutions (IFIs) are always trying to instrumentalize the participation of civil society according to their own interests.

Effective participation requires specific information and the knowledge to use it. It is therefore necessary that all documents relating to debt – especially from the IMF, World Bank and other IFIs – be published.

The participation of civil society should focus on excluded sectors and encourage the participation of parliaments and local governments in order to create the conditions for a more representative and transparent arbitration process. Some countries have a very weak civil society, which requires the support of civil society in other countries.

Assuring Compliance with a Debt Arbitration Verdict

The IMF has to play the same role as any other creditor. To ensure compliance with an arbitration verdict, social monitoring will be very important. Monitoring by civil society must be guaranteed.

Parliaments and Alliances

Parliamentarians must be informed and sensitized about arbitration. At present, some parliaments are far more controlled by their executive governments than others, and some parliaments have a more precise knowledge of the concept of arbitration than others. Parliamentarians (national and international) should be called upon to establish an international parliamentary working group on external debt and financial architecture. There should be a meeting of this working group in the near future. Strategic alliances should be sought with trade unions, the Interamerican Platform on Human Rights, the African Social Forum, the American Association of Lawyers, ecological groups, etc.

5

Eliminate All Illegitimate Debts – Be They for Weapons, Palaces or Useless Power Plants

Kairos – Canada

Even as fighting was raging in Baghdad, US Deputy Defence Secretary Paul Wolfowitz declared that the people of Iraq should not be saddled with debts incurred by Saddam Hussein 'to buy weapons and to build palaces' (Blustein 2003). Critics were quick to point out the cynicism behind these comments, since Russia, France and Germany, all opponents of the war, are Iraq's major northern creditors. Nevertheless, debt campaigners recognize that if the principle of cancelling 'odious debts' contracted by oppressive dictatorships were applied broadly, it would lead to the writing off of the illegitimate debts of many other countries.

While the world's media has focused on the invasion of Iraq, little attention has been given to the ongoing crisis in Sub-Saharan Africa, where under-funded healthcare services cannot provide treatment for 29.4 million people living with HIV/AIDS. Meanwhile, cash-strapped African governments pay around US$4 billion a year more in debt service than they receive in new loans (World Bank 2002).

Despite the 24 million signatures gathered worldwide by the Jubilee debt remission movement demanding the cancellation of poor countries' debts, their peoples remain trapped in debt bondage. Severely indebted low-income countries paid out US$14.4 billion more in interest and principle in 2000 than they received in new loans. For all developing countries taken together, the net outflow amounted to US$127.5 billion that same year (World Bank 2002).

This chapter will update supporters of the Jubilee debt movement on the failure of the official Heavily Indebted Poor Countries (HIPC) initiative to meet our demands. It will go on to deepen our analysis of the illegitimacy of developing countries' debts, drawing on recent studies by legal scholars, and examine the implications of the doctrine of 'odious debts'. It will argue that the doctrine should be applied not only in the case of Iraq, but also to many other countries' debts. Some of the options for achieving the cancellation of illegitimate debts under international law will be examined, as will calls for establishing an international debt arbitration tribunal as one way, among others, for eliminating illegitimate debts.

HIPC HAS FAILED TO DELIVER ON ITS PROMISES

Twenty-four million citizens from around the world signed petitions demanding the cancellation of low-income developing countries' external debts. Instead of listening to this unprecedented cry for justice, the leaders of the Group of Seven (G7), and the international financial institutions (IFIs) they control, responded by making only minor changes to their HIPC initiative.

The HIPC initiative emerged in 1996 after the IFIs themselves recognized that much of the debt owed by low-income countries was uncollectable. It was always a creditors' plan, with the limited goal of 'bringing debt down to sustainable levels, subject to satisfactory policy performance' (World Bank 2003: 11). From the beginning, the goal was never to eliminate the debt, but only to make debt payments 'sustainable'. Sustainability was defined arbitrarily as debts that are no more than 200–250 per cent as large as a country's annual exports.

The HIPC initiative was tied to a country's acceptance of orthodox structural adjustment conditions. In fact, it was another way of forcing countries that were not eligible for new loans because of their 'debt overhang' to accept more structural adjustment in return for some debt relief. The Canadian Jubilee campaign directly challenged this aspect of HIPC by demanding not just 100 per cent cancellation of all low-income countries' debts, but also an end to structural adjustment programmes (SAPs).

At its 1999 summit in Köln, Germany, the G7 responded to the Jubilee debt petition with its own Köln Debt Initiative. It called for some additional resources for the HIPC initiative and for 'a framework for poverty reduction' to be 'integrated with structural adjustment programmes' (G7 Finance Ministers 1999). This actually led to increased intervention by the IFIs into areas of domestic social policies previously untouched by SAPs.

Afterwards, the International Monetary Fund (IMF) and World Bank came up with a new 'enhanced HIPC'. Its essence remained the same, but its goals were restated as 'to provide a permanent exit from rescheduling [and] to free up resources for higher social spending aimed at poverty reduction' (World Bank 2003). Sustainability was redefined as debts only 150 per cent as large as exports, instead of 200-250 per cent.

The obligation that countries must have a three-year track record of adherence to IMF-approved macro-economic policies involving fiscal austerity and anti-inflationary monetary policies did not change. What was new was that governments had to produce Poverty Reduction Strategy Papers (PRSPs) indicating what additional measures would be undertaken to alleviate poverty without ever challenging the macro-economic policies which are a major cause of poverty in the first place.

The IMF and World Bank's own reports chronicle how the HIPC initiative has been a failure, even on its own terms:

- Only about one-third of the US$100 billion in debt relief promised at the Köln summit had actually been delivered as of March 2003. A precise accounting is not possible due to incomplete reporting by the G7, the IMF and the World Bank. However, it appears that so far they have delivered about US$12.5 billion of traditional debt cancellation (i.e. amounts that would have been written off even if there had been no HIPC initiative); about US$15 billion for eight HIPCs under the original and enhanced HIPC initiatives; US$1.3 billion in additional bilateral relief and perhaps US$3 billion in write-offs of Official Development Assistance loans.
- As of March 2003, only 26 out of an original list of 42 countries had qualified for the enhanced HIPC initiative.

- If all 26 countries eventually complete the HIPC process, then about US$41.5 billion of nominal debt relief will be provided through the HIPC initiative. Taking into account traditional debt relief that would have been accorded had HIPC never existed, additional bilateral relief and conversions of Official Development Assistance loans into grants, the total amount of debt relief might be equivalent to about one-fifth of all severely indebted low-income countries' long-term debts.
- What is worse is that four countries (Chad, Honduras, Niger and Zambia) will have annual debt service payments due in 2003–5 which will actually be higher than their annual debt services paid in 1998–2001.
- Of the 26 countries qualifying under HIPC, only seven have reached the 'completion point', when they are supposed to have achieved a lasting exit from 'unsustainable' debt burdens.
- Three of these seven countries – Uganda, Mauritania and Burkina Faso – still had 'unsustainable' debt burdens even after receiving the full HIPC treatment.
- The other 19 countries are in an 'interim' period, having qualified for some debt relief, but are still under the supervision of IMF and World Bank SAPs.
- Over half of these 19 countries have had their HIPC debt relief delayed because they fell 'off track' at some point; that is, they were not in compliance with some of the stiff austerity and structural adjustment conditions laid down by the Bank and the Fund. After a country falls 'off track', its deadline for 'graduating' from HIPC gets pushed into the future.
- According to IMF projections, even after these countries get back 'on track', only about half of them will have 'sustainable' debt burdens at their completion points.

The overall conclusion is that HIPC has been a failure, even on its own terms. One reason for this failure is the unrealistic projections of economic growth and of commodity export earnings the IMF and the World Bank used to calculate how much debt relief would be needed to achieve 'sustainability'.

If the enhanced HIPC did not deliver debt sustainability, did it at least free some money for social spending? A study by the North–South Institute found that the actual amount of debt service payments freed for the countries surveyed is equivalent to only 12.4 per cent of their already meagre annual social spending. In other words, these countries can increase their grossly inadequate spending on education, health and other social services by only one-eighth, due to the paltry amount of debt relief they will receive over the years 2001–15 (Serieux 2001).

HIPC contrasts with the treatment of Germany after the Second World War

At the end of the Second World War, the Allied powers gave West Germany a historically unprecedented postwar debt settlement. Instead of demanding reparations (as they had after the First World War), Britain, France and the United States decided that it was in their own best interests to give West Germany a generous settlement in order to revive its economy. In February 1953 the Allies signed the historic London Debt Accord with Germany that cancelled about half of a US$7.5 billion debt (worth about US$45 billion today) and rescheduled the rest over a long term at fixed interest rates. Moreover, Germany was only required to devote a maximum of 3 per cent of its export earnings to debt service and was even allowed to suspend debt service if it had a trade deficit.

In contrast, under the HIPC initiative, low-income countries must spend an average of 8.6 per cent of their export earnings on debt service and are not allowed to suspend payments even at the expense of paying for essential imports.

The sad reality is that many of the poorest countries in the world remain caught in the debt trap despite the promises made by IFIs. At the 2002 G8 summit in Kananaskis, Alberta, media reports talked about 'an additional US$1 billion in debt relief'. In fact this billion-dollar promise does not involve any new debt relief. It simply represents G7 contributions to the HIPC Trust Fund. The Trust Fund makes payments back to the World Bank and the IMF on behalf of low-income countries who otherwise would be unable to service their debts. It thus keeps up the fiction that no country ever defaults on loans from the World Bank and the IMF.

Canada's share of this top-up for the HIPC Trust Fund amounts to Cdn$75 million, which was delivered in the February 2003 budget. Adding more dollars to this fund will not result in any more debt relief for low-income countries, but it does constitute a bailout for the World Bank and the IMF. Instead of dipping into the Trust Fund, the IMF and World Bank should be obliged to write-off debts by using their own loan loss reserves, retained earnings and gold stocks.

In 1999–2000 the IMF sold 12.9 million ounces of its gold reserves, earning US$2.9 billion to finance its share of the HIPC initiative. The Fund still has another 103.4 million ounces of gold at its disposal, with a market value in early June 2003 of about US$37.5 billion. As of 30 June 2002, the World Bank had loan loss provisions of US$4.1 billion, as well as US$22.2 billion worth of 'retained earnings' on its books. If these IFIs operated like private sector lenders they would have to use their loan loss reserves and their retained earnings (which they would call 'profits') to write off bad debts.

The Canadian Ecumenical Jubilee Initiative, whose campaign has been taken up by Kairos, continues to demand the immediate cancellation of 100 per cent of all bilateral and multilateral debts. The IMF and the World Bank must absorb the costs through the sale of gold reserves and drawing down loan loss reserves and retained earnings.

Zambia: Committing mass murder by complacency

> The HIV/AIDS crisis is not a crisis of lack of resources. It is a crisis of lack of conscience. It is the obscene gap between the haves and have-nots that is driving this holocaust. (Lewis 2003)

In 2002, Kairos published a study on Zambia's debt crisis in preparation for the G8 summit in Kananaskis. At that summit, G8 leaders encouraged other creditor countries, the World Bank and the IMF to speed up the delivery of debt relief, especially for African countries. The G8 leaders also offered support for the New Partnership for Africa's Development (NEPAD), an economic programme for Africa's recovery and development.

NEPAD calls for greater integration of Africa into the global economy: 'The objective is to bridge existing gaps between Africa and the developed countries so as to improve the continent's international competitiveness and to enable her to participate in the globalization process' (NEPAD 2001, para. 98). The key priority of NEPAD is to attract foreign direct investment in energy, agriculture, communications, and human resources and to put in place the conditions to enable this investment to come to Africa.

In order to achieve the ambitious development and growth targets on their own in the long term, African leaders are asking for significant increases in aid and debt relief to the tune of US$64 billion per year. While the analysis of Africa's problems has some merit, the proposed solutions are deeply flawed. As the statement by African participants in a civil society gathering organized by the Canadian International Development Agency in May 2002 declared: 'The economic strategy at the heart of the NEPAD is based on the discredited package of IMF/World Bank-inspired economic policies that have been implemented by African countries for the past two decades with disastrous effects for their economies.'

Since the 2002 G8 summit, the plight of Africa has virtually fallen off the G8 leaders' table. At their 2003 summit in Evian, France, the leaders received a report on past efforts, but made few new pledges. There were no new announcements to enhance debt relief, as leaders continued to insist that the HIPC initiative is working and simply needs more fine-tuning.

Furthermore, there was no progress on the issue of allowing African countries to produce or import cheaper anti-retroviral medicine for HIV/AIDS and other life-threatening diseases. France had produced a draft declaration proposing better access to generic drugs, improved access to brand-name drugs through differential pricing and stimulating local production and technology transfer. But 'most of these measures were expunged from the final version at the insistence of the United States' because they threatened the intellectual property rights of transnational pharmaceutical companies (Tagliabue and Bumiller 2003).

France did announce an increase in its own commitment to the Global Fund for AIDS, Malaria and Tuberculosis from 50 million euros to 150 million euros (US$177 million) a year. France also promised to try to persuade an upcoming European Union Summit to contribute US$1.2 billion a year, but Canada failed to announce any increase in its paltry US$25 million annual contribution. Overall, the Global Fund remains woefully under funded.

For many of the poorest countries, the dismal response of the richer nations and the IFIs to the debt crisis has stalled any meaningful efforts toward recovery. In Zambia, the lack of progress is having a particularly deadly impact. In a region wracked by drought and ravaged by the HIV/AIDS pandemic, Zambia should be using all of its available financial resources to support its social infrastructure, as well as investing in food production. Zambians will see absolutely no real benefits from having some of their debts cancelled through the HIPC initiative. In fact, Zambia will be paying more in debt servicing between 2003–5 than it was paying prior to reaching its HIPC decision point in December of 2000 (see table below; Source: International Development Association, 2003).

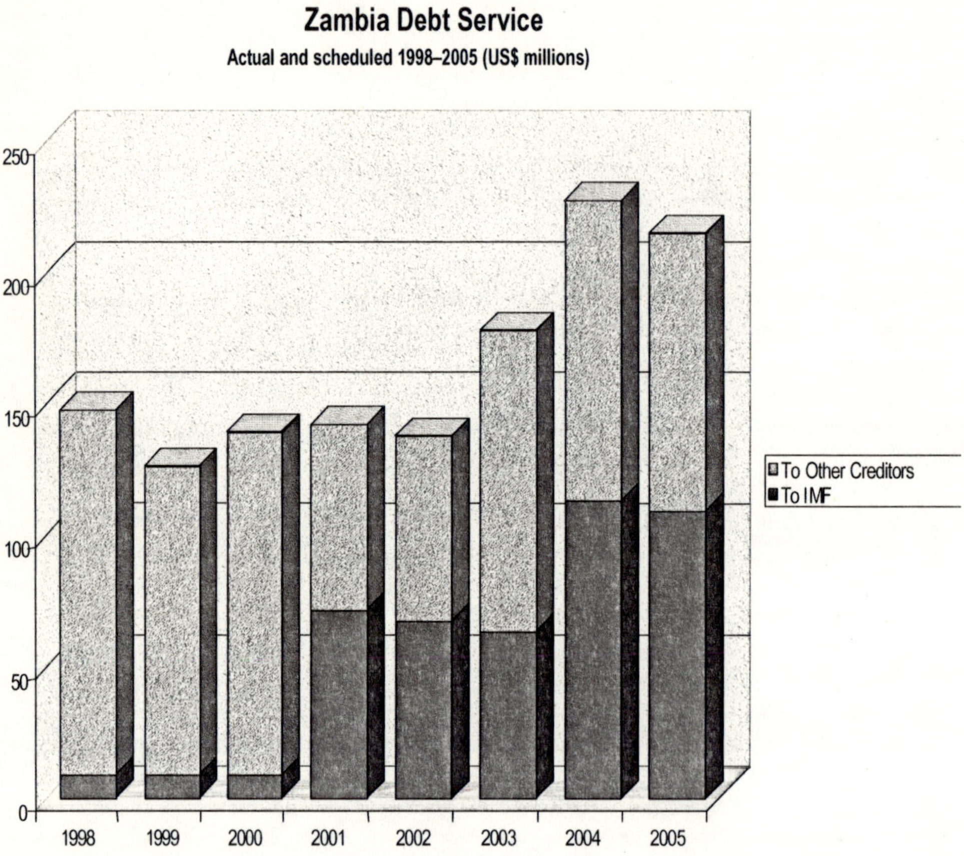

- Zambia's debt servicing commitments will increase by almost 50 per cent from an average of $138 million for the period 1998–2002 to an average of $207 million between 2003–5.
- After increasing from $9 million to $71 million between 2000 and 2001, Zambia's debt servicing requirements to the IMF will almost double between 2003 and 2004, from $63 million to $113 million.

Stephen Lewis (2003), the UN special envoy for HIV/AIDS in Africa, decried the lack of resources to address the HIV/Aids pandemic as 'mass murder by complacency'. Seen in this light, not only is the IMF guilty of complacency in the case of Zambia, it is also guilty of exacerbating the plight of Zambians by exacting $285 million in debt servicing over the next three years. What is worse is that

Zambians are being forced into these additional payments largely as a result of misguided policies imposed by the World Bank and IMF throughout the 1990s.

The HIV/AIDS pandemic is having a particularly harsh impact in Zambia. Life expectancy has plummeted from 54 years just a few years ago to 37 years and is expected to go as low as 30 years in the coming decade. Over 2,000 teachers died in 2002; only 1,000 graduated from Teacher's College. Many children cannot go to school because their parents have died and they can no longer afford the school fees. In this context, does it make any sense for the IMF to continue to bleed the country dry in order to balance its ledger sheet?

As of 1999, 238 of 311 state-owned firms in Zambia had been privatized, with about 100,000 workers losing their jobs. Employment in the formal sector of the economy fell from 566,000 in 1985 to 478,000 in 1999, affecting women and girls in particular. The negative impact also spilled over into the informal sector. Local businesses have collapsed and there has been a significant rise in unemployment and poverty (Njoroge 2001).

Instead of admitting its responsibility and liability in creating and exacerbating Zambia's debt crisis, the IMF instead remains fixated on recklessly forcing the country to continue selling off its remaining assets. Having privatized most of its mines and other public assets over the past decade, the IMF has now targeted Zambia's National Bank (Zanaco) and the public electric utility (Zesco) for privatization. According to the World Bank's Zambia country manager, Laurence Clarke, Zambia will not reach the completion point of the debt relief programme, 'if it does not privatize Zesco, Zamtel, Zanaco and these things have to be done quickly' (Manoah 2002)

There will be no additional debt relief, however paltry, until the sale of these assets is completed, despite mounting public opposition due to corruption scandals surrounding previous privatizations. The privatization of the National Bank will have an especially negative impact on women, as the privatized bank will move to close down access to its services in the less profitable rural areas and to those engaged in small-scale farming or business, the majority of whom are women (Longwe 2003).

> Zambia is like a country at war with tens of thousands of its people marginalized by the economic and social effects of poverty and deprivation of various forms and all linked to the external debt. (Jubilee Zambia)

In light of the worsening situation, Jubilee Zambia continues to call for the following measures:

- Totally cancelling Zambia's debts as a basis for a 'fresh start' to national recovery.
- Delinking debt cancellation from the imposition of macro-economic reforms and forced privatization of key industries.
- Financing poverty reduction and development through grants rather than loans.

DEEPENING OUR ANALYSIS OF ILLEGITIMATE DEBTS

Campaigners for the annulment of illegitimate debts recognize that the Bush administration's call for the annulment of Iraq's debts is an unwitting acknowledgement of the contemporary validity of the doctrine of 'odious debts', which holds that citizens must not be obliged to honour debts contracted by oppressive dictatorships. The doctrine of odious debts was first applied following another US military conquest: the occupation of Cuba during the Spanish-American War of 1898. Following that war, the US refused to honour Cuba's debts with Spain, on the grounds that the Cuban people had no voice in contracting loans used to suppress their bid for independence.

G8 discord over Iraqi debt

Early calls by US Treasury Secretary John Snow and Deputy Defence Secretary Paul Wolfowitz for substantial write-offs of Iraqi debt were met with anger and hostility on the part of other G8 nations. Critics were quick to point out that not only is the US not a major Iraqi creditor, but it also has plans to use revenue from Iraqi oil sales to finance reconstruction projects managed by US firms with close ties to the Bush administration.

The task of reaching a consensus on what to do about Iraqi debt is complicated by the absence of reliable data, since Iraq is one of only a handful of countries that did not participate in the World Bank's debt reporting system. Its debts are variously estimated at between US$60 billion and US$127 billion, not including US$199 billion due in reparations to Kuwait and other countries arising from the first Gulf War and outstanding contracts for petroleum development services worth US$57 billion. While neighbouring Middle Eastern states are Iraq's major creditors, Germany and France are reportedly owed about US$4 billion each. Germany's finance minister rejected Snow's suggestion that Iraq's debts be cancelled, saying: 'I don't merely expect to get the $4 billion back - I will get it back' (Beattie 2003a).

Russia is reportedly owed between US$8 billion and US$12 billion and is said to have outstanding contracts signed with Iraq for petroleum industry development worth US$52 billion. In response to Snow's suggestion, Russia's finance minister angrily retorted: 'No one has forgiven Russia's debt regardless of what kind of regime it was' (Beattie 2003a). Ever since the fall of the Soviet Union, Russia has argued to no avail that debts accumulated during the Soviet era should also be deemed odious.

Unable to agree among themselves on immediate debt write-offs, it appears that the G8 reached a political compromise during the period prior to their 2003 summit. It seems that the G8 agreed to defer decisions on Iraqi debt until 2004, when a new government would be installed in Iraq which will be subject to a SAP designed by the IMF.

At the April 2003 meeting of the G7 finance ministers (Russia is not invited to these meetings, although it is now a full member at the G8 leaders' summits), the Europeans strongly resisted pressure to cancel Iraqi debts outright. Instead, the G7 issued a bland communiqué saying only that Iraq's debts would be referred to the Paris Club of government creditors. At their May 2003 meeting in Deauville,

France, the finance ministers again discussed Iraqi debt without coming to any final agreement. Their communiqué does not even mention Iraq by name, but instead calls for new flexibility on the part of the Paris Club, implying that there might be some special political treatment for Iraq.

The effect of referring Iraq's debts to the Paris Club is that Iraq is unlikely to make any debt payments until the end of 2004 at the earliest. Before the Paris Club can decide on even a partial debt write-down, a new Iraqi government will have to agree to an IMF SAP.

Eric Toussaint (2003) charges that the G7 'agreed to set Iraq's foreign debt at US$120 billion … not [including] the compensation owed by Iraq for the invasion of Kuwait.' Toussaint calculates that with the amount owed for compensation to Kuwait and outstanding contracts added in, Iraq's total debt would reach US$380 billion, which is larger than the US$320 billion dollars owed by Brazil, hitherto the South's largest debtor. Toussaint concludes: 'The arbitrary agreement on this amount is directly aimed at justifying the take-over of Iraq's oil resources on the pretext of ensuring the repayment of the debt. Fixing the debt so high has the enormous advantage of subjecting the new Iraqi authorities to the demands of the creditors for decades.'

According to the Russian newspaper Izvestia, Russia traded off its support for a UN Security Council motion recognizing the US and Britain as occupying powers in Iraq, with control over its oil revenues, for a commitment that at least some of Russia's debt claims and oil service contracts will be respected (Agence France Presse 2003). When Presidents Bush and Putin met in St. Petersburg before the Evian G8 summit, they discussed how Iraq's oil contracts would be apportioned.

While the final contours of a settlement are not yet known, it seems clear that the major powers intend to decide on the use of Iraqi oil revenues and on the final disposition of its foreign debts by wheeling and dealing among themselves without reference to the will of the Iraqi people or the principles of international law.

The classic definition of odious debts was articulated by international legal scholar Alexander Sack at the beginning of the twentieth century:

> If a despotic power incurs a debt not for the needs or in the interest of the state, but to strengthen its despotic regime, to repress the population that fights against it … This debt is odious to the population of all the state. The debt is not an obligation for the nation; it is a regime's debt, a personal debt of the power that has incurred it, consequently it falls with the fall of this power. (Cited in Khalfan et al. 2002)

Clearly, the debts incurred by Saddam Hussein to buy arms and build palaces fit within this definition. So do the debts incurred by the Ferdinand Marcos dictatorship in the Philippines. It is estimated that Marcos took some US$5-13 billion with him when he fled into exile in 1986. Similarly, Mobutu Sese Seko, who ruled Zaire (now the Democratic Republic of Congo) with an iron fist from 1965 to 1989, looted billions of dollars from the national treasury. Even after the IMF's own appointee, Erwin Blumenthal, resigned in disgust from running Zaire's central bank in 1979 because of the rampant corruption, the IMF loaned Mobutu another US$700 million. The World Bank lent Zaire another US$2 billion over the next 15 years, all because Mobutu was deemed to be a Western ally in the Cold War. Yet 'the US did not protest when the IMF greeted the downfall of Mobutu by suggesting that whatever new government was established should get working on its $14 billion external debt' (Ambrose and Njehu 2003).

As described in detail in our March 2002 Global Economic Justice Report, Argentina's debt rose over four-fold during the period of military dictatorship from 1976 to 1983. It is estimated that the Argentine Generals spent some US$13.9 billion on arms purchases while they pursued a 'dirty war' in which 30,000 Argentines were either killed or 'disappeared'. Clearly, a substantial part of Argentina's present debt is odious and must not be paid. Similarly, the billions of dollars borrowed by the apartheid regime in South Africa to finance the police and military repression of the black majority must be accounted as odious debt. The table below provides estimates of odious debts contracted by some well-known dictatorships.

Redifining Odious Debt

The Centre for International Sustainable Development Law (CISDL) at McGill University has produced a study entitled 'Advancing the Odious Debt Doctrine'. The study examines the historical application of the doctrine of odious debts and concludes that there are sound legal arguments for extending the definition of odious debt beyond cases of overt dictatorships. Whereas a narrow definition would only apply to certain debts contracted by despotic regimes, the CISDL study argues cogently for the following broad definition: 'Odious debts are those contracted against the interests of the population of a state, without its consent and with the full awareness of the creditor' (Khalfan et al. 2002)

Thus, odious debts, broadly defined, have three criteria. The first - that loans did not benefit the population - would cover many more development loans than one might first expect. For example, the World Bank's own evaluation unit found that between 60-70 per cent of the projects it undertook in low-income countries in South Asia and Africa during the 1990s had failed.

The second criterion - absence of consent by the population - is most easily demonstrated in the cases of dictators' debts. In other instances, an inquiry into the circumstances under which each credit was contracted may be needed to determine whether democratic procedures were followed. Legal precedents exist for the repudiation of certain debts, as contracted by the US states of North Carolina, South Carolina and Mississippi in the nineteenth century, on the grounds that they 'were tainted with fraud, served personal enrichment rather than public purposes, and were contracted in the absence of proper authority' (Khalfan et al. 2002)

The third criterion, which requires that creditors be aware of what happened to the money they lent, would not allow creditors wilfully to turn a blind eye to how their loans were used.

After examining various principles of international and domestic law, judicial decisions and the writings of international law experts, the CISDL study concludes: 'There are legally persuasive arguments in favour of the morally compelling doctrine of odious debt' (Khalfan et al. 2002)

Table: Some cases of odious debts (Source: Hanlon, 2002:49)

Country	**Dictatorship**	**Odious debts (US$ billions)**
Indonesia	Suharto	126
Brazil	Military junta	100
Argentina	Military junta	65
Philippines	Marcos	40
Syria	Assad	22
South Africa	Apartheid	22
Pakistan	Military	19
Sudan	Nimeiry/al-Mahdi	17
Thailand	Military	14
Nigeria	Buhari/Abacha	14
Chile	Pinochet	13
Zaire/DRC	Mobutu	13
Algeria	Military	5
Iran	Shah	5
Kenya	Moi	4
Ethiopia	Mengistu	4
Bolivia	Military junta	3
Somalia	Siad Barre	2
Paraguay	Stroessner	2
Malawi	Banda	2
El Salvador	Military junta	1
Liberia	Doe	1
Haiti	Duvalier	1

Debts for destructive projects

The expanded definition of odious debt would then include many kinds of debts first identified at a forum sponsored by the Canadian Ecumenical Jubilee Initiative in November 2000 as illegitimate on the grounds that they were contracted for fraudulent purposes, did not benefit the people or were destructive to the community or the environment. Examples of debts incorporating one or more of these elements abound. Perhaps the classic case is the US$2.2 billion debt incurred by the Philippines between 1976 and 1985 to build the Bataan nuclear power plant. The nuclear reactor has never operated because it was built on an earthquake faultline near a volcano. Westinghouse, which built the plant, has admitted that it paid a commission, estimated at US$80 million, to a Marcos associate to win the contract, despite a lower bid from General Electric.

Consider what might have happened if this project had been built in the US. In 1984 the US Supreme Court ruled that five municipalities in Idaho did not have to honour debts contracted for a failed nuclear power project. Like the Bataan plant, two nuclear reactors built by the Washington State Public Power Supply System failed to deliver electricity. The Supreme Court upheld an Idaho State court decision that the cities' agreement to help finance the nuclear plants had not been authorized by local voters and therefore violated the state constitution. At US$43 million, it was the largest municipal bond default to date in US history. Yet the principal financier for the Bataan project, the US government's own Ex-Im Bank and other creditors, still demand that the Philippines pay US$170,000 a day on a debt that will not be paid off until 2018.

There are countless examples of projects that not only failed to deliver benefits but also had negative social and environmental effects. Among the most notorious are large hydro dams, mines and pipelines. Many of these projects led to the displacement of local communities and disruption of local ecosystems, thus adding to the huge ecological debts that northern creditors owe to southern peoples. Despite these disastrous consequences, creditors still demand that southern peoples pay these debts when in fact it is the North that should be paying compensation to the South (see Economic Justice Report, 2000.)

Debts which cannot be repaid without harming people and communities

Another category of illegitimate debts includes those whose repayment would cause harm to people and their communities. This category would apply to states that are unable to meet the basic needs of their people, including the right to healthcare - a violation of their fundamental human rights. Consider the situation in Sub-Saharan Africa, where 2.4 million people died from HIV/AIDS in 2002, over three-quarters of all deaths worldwide. Another 29.4 million Africans are living with HIV (UNAIDS). African states need an additional US$10 billion a year for resources to fight HIV/AIDS and other infectious diseases that are devastating their populations. Yet in 2000, despite some debt service reductions under the HIPC initiative, Sub-Saharan African states paid US$4.8 billion more in debt service payments than they received in new loans. In 2001 their debt payments exceeded new lending by another US$3.1 billion (World Bank 2002).

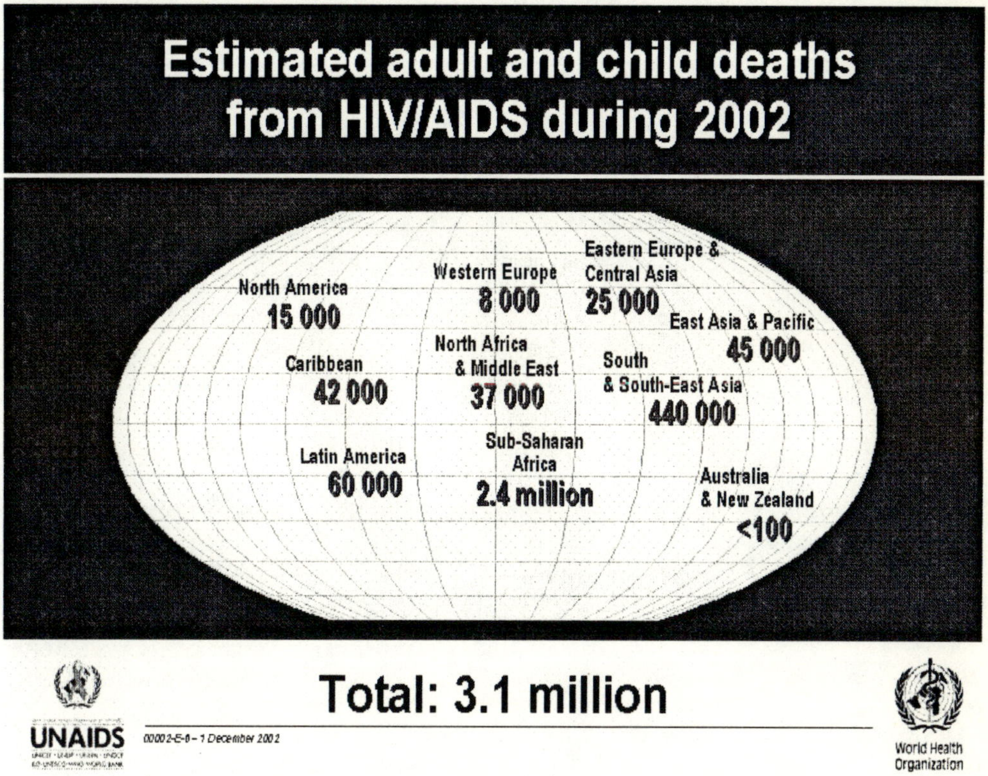

The example of Zambia (see earlier) illustrates why low-income developing countries must have 100 per cent of their debts cancelled immediately.

Debts that became illegitimate due to factors beyond debtors' control

Another group of illegitimate debts includes those that may have been legitimate when initially contracted, but whose servicing costs rose uncontrollably due to external factors over which the borrowing states had no control. A prime example is what happened to bank loans contracted at floating interest rates during the 1970s. These loan contracts committed the borrowers to pay interest rates that were marginally above other rates - usually the US prime rate or a measure called LIBOR (the London Inter-Bank Offered Rate). Thus the actual rates charged would move up or down depending on what happened on money markets in the US or the UK.

Many Latin American governments contracted floating rate loans in the 1970s, when rates were low, only to find their repayment costs skyrocket in the 1980s after the US raised interest rates. In 1979 the average interest rate on floating rate loans to Latin American governments was 6.25 per cent. When the US raised interest rates dramatically, rates on other world financial markets rose as well. By 1981 the average interest rate for loans to Latin America had soared to a ridiculous 24 per cent (Arruda 2000a). This unilateral increase in interest rates cost Latin America an extra US$106 billion in interest payments between 1978 and 1985.

The restructuring of the US economy away from production in favour of financial speculation contributed to a fall in demand for primary commodities on which most developing countries depend for export earnings. The net result was that the real interest rates paid by third world countries (nominal rates adjusted for falling commodity prices) averaged 14.6 per cent between 1981 and 1986, a huge increase over the 1-1.5 per cent average prevailing prior to 1980.

Although African countries, unlike their Latin American counterparts, had few floating interest rate loans, they too were devastated by the fall in commodity prices. Over the 1980s, average commodity prices fell by almost two-fifths, a trend that was especially devastating for a region that relies more on low value-added agricultural and mineral exports than other regions. More recently, African countries have once again been overwhelmed by another decline in commodity prices. Between 1997 and 2001, copper prices fell by 27 per cent, cotton by 39 per cent and coffee by 66 per cent. Opa Kapifimpanga (2003: 2) cites World Bank data showing that losses due to falling terms of trade (export prices in relation to import prices) are currently costing Sub-Saharan Africa US$60 billion a year. Yet African countries are still being obliged to keep up payments on their foreign debts.

Annulling debts on the basis of force majeure

Hugo Ruiz Diaz, a Paraguayan lawyer with a doctorate in international law, argues that an exception to the legal obligation to pay debts can be established in cases where debts become unpayable due to factors beyond the control of debtor governments. He argues for suspending debt payments on the grounds of force majeure - the legal doctrine that holds that external factors can make it impossible to fulfil a contract. Ugarteche and Acosta (2003: 32) argue for the insertion of force majeure clauses into international credit contracts that are analogous to those that already exist in contracts for the delivery of goods. For example, when Steelworkers Local 6500 went on strike against Inco in Sudbury, the company declared force majeure on contracts it had signed for deliveries of nickel, copper and cobalt.

Ugarteche and Acosta (2003) argue force majeure could be invoked when debts grow exponentially after a unilateral increase in interest rates, when loans cannot be paid because of an unforeseen drop in commodity prices and when debts are rendered unpayable because of a speculative attack against a nation's currency. Another potential reason for invoking force majeure could be the unforeseen drop in production that is occurring in Africa because people with HIV/AIDS are too sick to work.

Ruiz Diaz also argues that inappropriate economic policies imposed on a state by the IMF and the World Bank can be among the reasons for invoking force majeure. Such an action would reinforce an observation by the African Forum on

Debt and Development (AFRODAD) that some debts are illegitimate because they were incurred due to faulty policy advice. For example, the government of Mozambique, contrary to its own wishes, was forced to follow World Bank advice that led to the devastation of its cashew nut industry in order to obtain loans from the Bank and other creditors. The World Bank later admitted that its advice was wrong, but only after much of the cashew nut industry had been ruined. Mozambique was left saddled with an unjust debt which it should not be compelled to pay.

OPTIONS FOR ACTION

In light of the refusal of the G8 and the IFIs to act decisively, a number of diverse but complementary strategies must be pursued to attain the goals of the Jubilee debt remission movement: the unconditional, 100 per cent cancellation of all illegitimate debts.

As a basic principle, we must reiterate our support for the sovereign right of debtor countries to refuse to pay illegitimate debts. We must stand in solidarity with all peoples who choose to repudiate illegitimate debts, demanding that they not be denied trade financing or official development assistance. In addition, there are a variety of other actions that could be taken to achieve the annulment of illegitimate debts. Here we will consider first some possibilities for using international courts and United Nations bodies to challenge illegitimate external debts.

One course of action could be to use international courts to establish a modern precedent for determining whether vast amounts of third world debts are indeed odious and therefore must be cancelled outright. The CISDL study suggests actions that go beyond the merely opportunistic invocation of the doctrine of odious debt to measures that would establish the illegitimacy of perhaps the majority of third world debts.

To achieve this outcome, political action, including the mobilizing of public opinion, is needed to familiarize people with a broad definition of odious debt and to persuade an influential international judicial body to support a modern interpretation of the doctrine. This could be an important step towards the creation of an international tribunal to assess and cancel odious debts.

Both judicial and human rights bodies could be used

Although various judicial bodies could be approached to give legitimacy to the doctrine of odious debt, the CISDL study suggests that the International Court of Justice (ICJ) in the Hague 'is probably the ideal eventual forum [since] its judges are relatively independent of any one state and more likely to be open to non-traditional arguments' (Khalfan et al. 2002). To take a test case to the ICJ, normally both the lender and the creditor state must consent to the court's jurisdiction. One scenario might involve a test case brought to the ICJ with the consent of a sympathetic creditor state.

Another option is for the United Nations General Assembly, with the support of at least 60 states, to take a case to the ICJ. Civil society groups succeeded in winning General Assembly support for a case during the campaign against nuclear weapons. Alternatively, a UN agency such as the World Health Organization, the

Food and Agricultural Organization or the International Labour Organization can request an advisory opinion from the ICJ.

International human rights law provides a basis for winning recognition that some debt payments are illegitimate due to the harm they cause to people and their communities. The United Nations Committee on Economic, Social and Cultural Rights has noted that debt payments can violate fundamental human rights when they deprive states of the ability to provide adequate nutrition, education, healthcare and other basic needs to their population. Every five years, the committee asks for reports on measures that states have taken to implement the International Covenant on Economic, Social and Cultural Rights.

The CISDL study notes that 'the Covenant lays an obligation on states to engage in international cooperation to the maximum of their available resources' (Khalfan et al. 2002). The committee is also a favourable venue for taking action in that it actively solicits opinions from civil society. Although the committee's opinions are not binding on its members, it can play an important role in building pressure for the annulment of illegitimate debts.

An international debt arbitration tribunal

Another option for action that many civil society organizations (CSOs) are calling for is the establishment of an international debt arbitration tribunal that would be empowered to order the cancellation of debts whose repayment violates people's human rights. University of Vienna Professor Kunibert Raffer (1992) has argued cogently for establishing such a tribunal modelled on Chapter Nine of US federal bankruptcy law.

Chapter Nine applies to municipal governments in the US and as such is a model of how an insolvency proceeding can be applied to a sovereign state. It combines a general framework with flexibility to deal with particular situations. Only a debtor government can initiate a procedure. Once a petition is filed under Chapter Nine, there is an automatic stay on enforcement of claims against the debtor. The most significant feature of Chapter Nine is that it exempts from creditors' reach resources needed by the municipality to meet the needs of its population. Thus a government is not expected to stop providing essential services for the health, safety and well-being of its people. Raffer expresses the essence of a tribunal's objective as follows:

> In a situation of over-indebtedness the right of creditors to interest and repayments collides with the principle recognized generally by all civilized legal systems that no one must be forced to fulfil contracts if that leads to inhumane distress, endangers one's life or health, or violates human dignity. Briefly put, debtors cannot be forced to starve themselves or their children to be able to pay … Human rights and human dignity of debtors are given priority over unconditional repayment. (Cited in Round 2003: 16)

Under Chapter Nine proceedings, the people affected have a chance to influence the outcome. For example, municipal employees may be represented through their trade unions. Under an international Chapter Nine procedure, CSOs would have a chance to testify concerning the devastating effects of debt on local populations.

An international debt arbitration tribunal would function on the basis of the appointment of an equal number of arbitrators (one or two) by the creditors and the debtor state to a panel whose members would then choose a neutral chairperson from a roster of qualified people. A public audit of the country's debts would have to take place before a panel could convene. The panel would then be empowered to order write-offs or write-downs of the debts, including those owed to the IMF or other IFIs. Only a debtor government could initiate an arbitration process. Its assets could no longer be seized by order of the creditor's court. Furthermore, a debtor would be eligible to receive new credits while the proceedings were underway.

Many questions remain unresolved concerning how and where such a tribunal might be established. Some proponents argue that ad hoc tribunals could be established on a case-by-case basis without any new institution or bureaucracy required. Others argue for setting up a tribunal within the United Nations. Some suggest that a new body should be established through an international treaty, while others say that an existing body like the Permanent Court of Arbitration (which has existed in the Hague since 1899) could be used (AFRODAD 2002b).

Cautious support

A more fundamental question, however, is whether an international arbitration tribunal is the best forum for judging and resolving all the complex issues concerning the legitimacy of external debts.

At the November 2000 forum on illegitimate debt sponsored by the Canadian Ecumenical Jubilee Initiative, Canadian church debt campaigners gave cautious, critical support to calls for the establishment of such a tribunal, subject to further research and analysis. The reason for our wariness was a concern that calls for an international tribunal might be co-opted through the establishment of a debt rescheduling mechanism that, like the HIPC initiative, would end up writing off only debts that could not be collected in the first place.

In particular, we stressed that a debt restructuring mechanism should not be established under the IMF or the World Bank, as these institutions are creditors in their own right and would use debt rescheduling to impose structural adjustment conditionality. Furthermore, these institutions are subject to manipulation by their most powerful member states, especially the United States. Finally, we had concerns that an international debt arbitration tribunal might result in the legitimizing of otherwise illegitimate debts by applying only narrow 'debt sustainability' criteria, as does the HIPC process.

In our analysis, a debt arbitration tribunal has potential as a place to determine how much debt must be written off when its repayment would constitute a violation of human rights. However, debt arbitrators would not necessarily have the expertise to judge other forms of illegitimacy involving debts contracted for fraudulent purposes, for failed products or without proper legal authority. It would be much more appropriate to take these kinds of debts to courts of law before approaching an arbitration tribunal. Alternatively, a sovereign debtor could approach an arbitration tribunal to win a payments write-down, without prejudice to a later court decision that some of its debts are odious and therefore null and void in their entirety. In short, a carefully designed arbitration tribunal could play a role in dealing with some kinds of illegitimate debts, but it should not be seen as a panacea.

Developments since 2000 have proven that we had every reason to be cautious. There is a world of difference between the kind of fair and transparent arbitration mechanism advocated by many NGOs and the plans for a Sovereign Debt Restructuring Mechanism (SDRM) that emerged during 2001 as a serious initiative from the IMF.

SDRM

The official debate on establishing an international mechanism for restructuring sovereign debt took off in earnest after President George W. Bush's first Treasury Secretary, Paul O'Neill, surprised his own staff by telling a US Congressional committee that he saw a need for 'an international Chapter Eleven' bankruptcy mechanism. (O'Neill had gained a reputation for plain speaking that cost him his job when President Bush replaced him with the more circumspect John Snow.)

True to his roots as an executive of the Aluminum Company of America, the model that O'Neill chose to emulate was not Chapter Nine, but Chapter Eleven, which applies to corporate bankruptcies. O'Neill came into the Treasury job declaring his dislike for the kind of massive IMF-led bailouts of foreign creditors that had characterized the Mexican financial crisis of 1994-5 and the Asian crisis of 1997-8. He had good reason to criticize huge bailout loans that nominally go to the governments of heavily indebted countries but in fact end up benefiting private lenders who get repaid first, leaving the debtor countries' citizens with even heavier debt burdens. Ever since the Asian crisis, government and IFI officials had debated how 'to involve the private sector' in debt restructurings. Effectively, this means making private lenders bear some of the costs of the crises they contributed to through overzealous, imprudent lending.

O'Neill's remarks provided an opportunity for Anne Krueger, a US academic economist nominated by the Bush administration to the post of first deputy director at the IMF, to advance her idea for a new SDRM closely linked to the IMF (Krueger 2001, 2002a, 2002b).

The essence of Krueger's proposal is for a mechanism to allow private creditors to negotiate a restructuring arrangement with the debtor government. It is not an arbitration process whereby a neutral third party helps to determine the details of a settlement. Under her plan, the IMF would retain its status as a 'preferred creditor' and thus would be exempt from having to make any write-downs and would continue to receive payments ahead of every other creditor (Krueger 2002a: 17). Krueger (2002b: 2) insists: 'Our goal is not to make default an easy way out, but rather to create better incentives for [debt] restructuring while protecting asset values and creditors' rights.'

In a comprehensive critique, Robin Round (2003) of the Halifax Initiative coalition exposes SDRM's major flaws and demonstrates how it is analogous to the failed HIPC initiative. She details the reasons why NGOs, campaigning for a fair and transparent arbitration mechanism, oppose SDRM as contrary to their fundamental goals. Debt campaigners, however, cannot take the credit for defeating SDRM, as it was also strongly opposed by private financial interests.

Wall Street rejected SDRM in favour of a 'market-based' approach

The initial response of large private financial corporations to Krueger's proposals was quite hostile. One Wall Street fund manager called her plan 'a complete non-starter.' Walter Wriston, the influential former chair of Citicorp, said: 'It's an idea that doesn't really have any relevance in the real world' (Altman 2002).

It appeared that the Krueger plan had suffered a premature death when US Treasury Undersecretary John Taylor shot it down, calling instead for a more 'market-oriented' approach not requiring the creation of a new institutional framework for negotiations. The essence of this approach involves writing 'collective action clauses' (CACs) into bond contracts. These clauses would allow groups representing the majority of the owners of a particular bond issue to negotiate with the debtor government. Any deal would then have to be approved by a 'supermajority' of bond owners, probably 70 or 80 per cent.

However, Taylor did not persuade his boss, Treasury Secretary O'Neill, to abandon SDRM. Some G7 governments continued to support it and soon communiqués from the G7 finance ministers called for the simultaneous pursuit of both SDRM and a market-oriented approach.

Then the International Institute of Finance (IIF), the leading association of private financial institutions, publicly admitted a change in policy as it embraced the market-oriented approach. The large financial institutions the IIF represents need a way to head off the so-called 'rogue creditors' and 'vulture funds'. These are small investment firms who buy up minority stakes in a country's foreign debts, often at a deep discount from their face value, and then take legal action to demand full payment. Such actions may result in the rogue creditors getting paid off first at the expense of larger institutions. Legal actions by minority bond holders might also trigger 'cross default clauses', forcing the larger creditors to undertake long and costly court battles that might be avoided through a renegotiation process. The IIF conceded that endorsing the market-based approach was in its members' interests, since CACs allow the largest players to negotiate together and use their majority voting power to keep smaller creditors in line.

The final demise of SDRM occurred only after John Snow replaced O'Neill as US Treasury secretary. At the April 2003 spring meetings of the IMF, SDRM was, in the words of journalist Alan Beattie (2003b), 'placed right at the back of the highest shelf that the long arm of the US Treasury could reach.' The market-based approach then became the norm, as first Mexico, then Brazil, South Africa and Uruguay, began to write CACs into new bond issues.

According to Beattie, the first test of the market-based approach is a deal that Uruguay struck with its private creditors in April 2003 to restructure its debts without the mediation of any restructuring mechanism or arbitrator. The deal involved reprogramming about half of Uruguay's US$11 billion debt into new bonds containing CACs.

Debt campaigners cannot discern anything new in Uruguay's settlement, as it closely resembles so much of the debt rescheduling of the past. The deal does not involve any actual reduction of debt stocks, just the lengthening of maturities while interest rates are left unchanged. While the arrangement offers some short-term relief, it only postpones the day of reckoning. The deal allows Uruguay to take out new loans from the IMF and World Bank which, as usual, come with stern structural adjustment conditions attached.

In short, after all the talk about establishing a new mechanism for debt rescheduling, the outcome is no different to past debt renegotiations. There is no hint of any effort to examine the legitimacy of Uruguay's debt, much of which originated under a brutal military dictatorship. For debt campaigners, it represents little more than a reprogramming of odious debts rather than their cancellation.

Certainly, the debate on the establishment of some kind of debt restructuring mechanism or arbitration tribunal has not ended. It is likely to heat up again the next time a sovereign government cannot meet its debt obligations. Therefore, debt campaigners must give careful thought as to how to advocate for effective debt cancellation mechanisms, in face of the ever-present danger of having our demands watered down and co-opted.

Avenues for action

A broad programme of action is needed to confront the complex challenges posed by so many diverse kinds of illegitimate debts. As Alejandro Bendaña (2002) of Jubilee South explains: 'The problem of external indebtedness will not be solved by arbitration alone.'

This chapter has suggested six avenues for actions to address the complex problem of illegitimate debts without relying solely on the creation of an international debt arbitration mechanism.

First, we must recognize that the citizens of debtor countries themselves are the major protagonists. We must reiterate our readiness to stand by all peoples who refuse to pay illegitimate debts. We can demonstrate our solidarity with them by exposing the failure of the HIPC initiative and demanding the unconditional cancellation of all low-income countries' debts held by the IFIs.

Second, the current situation arising from the invasion of Iraq creates an opportunity for the international Jubilee movement to demand that the doctrine of odious debt be taken seriously. This demand should involve the abolition of Iraq's odious debts, as well as all others. Debt campaigners should point to the many other examples of debts that originated under repressive dictatorships over the last half century. Annulment of Iraq's debts could set an important precedent.

Third, continued education and mobilization of public opinion is needed to build international support for approaching a judicial body, such as the ICJ, to win a modern precedent for annulling odious debts as they have been broadly defined in this chapter. Cases involving not just the debts incurred by dictatorships, but also those that came from failed projects that did not benefit the population or were contracted for fraudulent purposes, need to be taken to international tribunals like the ICJ in order to establish modern precedents for an expanded application of the doctrine of odious debts.

Fourth, cases demonstrating how debt repayments deprive populations of basic human rights should be presented to the UN Committee on Economic, Social and

Cultural Rights in order to build a body of evidence for recognizing the right to refuse to pay debts that violate basic human rights.

Fifth, national audits are needed to build the case against illegitimate debts and discern which debts are odious in the broad sense, which are illegitimate due to circumstances beyond the debtor's control and therefore subject to force majeure, and which are illegitimate because their repayment would violate basic human rights. Ideally, these audits should be conducted with the full resources and full disclosure of the debtor states and assistance from forensic accountants.

Civil society groups should demand that governments initiate these audits. One tactic for persuading states to exercise this responsibility is initiating citizens' audits, as is being done in Brazil. There, a Citizens' Audit of External Debt is combing through public records to determine the origins and the legitimacy of Brazil's external debt, which regimes contracted the original debts, whether they were used for a pubic purpose and whether they grew due to factors beyond Brazil's control.

Sixth, calls for establishing an international debt arbitration tribunal modelled on Chapter Nine of US bankruptcy law should continue with due vigilance concerning the danger of having such efforts co-opted through the reintroduction of a mechanism like SDRM.

Conclusion: Suggestions for Canadians

Citizens can write to the prime minister and finance minister to reiterate the demands of the Canadian churches' debt campaign:

1. Immediate and unconditional cancellation of 100 per cent of the bilateral and multilateral debts of all low-income countries, requiring the IMF to use its gold reserves and the World Bank to use its loan loss reserves and retained earnings to pay the costs.
2. An end to the imposition of Structural Adjustment Programmes and an end to the forced privatization of public assets as a condition for receiving debt cancellation.
3. Cooperation with measures that will lead to the cancellation of the illegitimate debts of all developing countries.

With millions of people dying every year from HIV/AIDS and other infectious diseases due to lack of funds for treatment, debt cancellation is more urgent than ever. To remain silent while thousands die daily is 'to commit mass murder by complacency'.

References

AFRODAD (2002a) 'Call for Establishment of a Fair and Transparent Arbitration Mechanism on debt', Policy Brief No.1. Harare: African Forum and Network on Debt and Development. www.afrodad.org.

AFRODAD (2002b) 'Fair and Transparent Arbitration on debt", Issues Paper

No.1. Harare: African Forum and Network on Debt and Development. www.afrodad.org.

AFRODAD (2002c) 'The Efficacy of Establishing an International Arbitration Court for Debt', Technical Paper No.1. Harare: African Forum and Network on Debt and Development. www.afrodad.org.

Agence France Presse (2003) 'Russia "sold" UN Iraq Vote for Oil and Debt.' Odiousdebts.org website, 23 May.

Altman, Daniel (2002) 'A Country in Chapter 11?' New York Times, 6 January.

Ambrose, Soren and Njehu, Njoki Njoroge (2003) 'The Second Invasion: The IMF, the World Bank, and Iraq.' In 50 Years Is Enough, Economic Justice Newsletter. US Network for Global Economic Justice.

Arruda, Marcos (2000a) External Debt: Brazil and the International Financial Crisis. London: Pluto Press.

Beattie, Alan (2003a) 'World Bank and IMF "Ready to Play Normal Role" in Iraq.' Financial Times, 14 April.

Beattie, Alan (2003b) 'Uruguay Provides Test Case for Merits of Voluntary Debt Exchange.' Financial Times, 23 April.

Bendaña, Alejandro (2002) 'Repudiation and Arbitration: The Need for an Integral Approach.' Jubilee South. www.jubileesouth.org.

Blustein, Paul (2003) 'US Plans for Iraqi Economy Hit Friction.' Washington Post, 11 April.

Cheru, Fantu (2000) 'Debt Relief and Social Investment: Linking the HIPC Initiative to the HIV/Aids Epidemic in Africa: The Case of Zambia.' Review of African Political Economy, Vol. 27, No. 86, 519-36.

Economic Justice Report (2000) 'Ecological Debt: South Tells North "Time to Pay Up,"' October.

G7 Finance Ministers (1999) Report of G7 Finance Ministers on the Köln Debt Initiative to the Köln Economic Summit, 18-20 June.

G7 Finance Ministers (2002) Statement of G7 Finance Ministers and Central Bank Governors and Action Plan, Washington DC, 20 April 20. Available at www.fin.gc.ca.

Halifax Initiative and Social Justice Committee (2003) 'Water, Land and Labour.'

Hanlon, Joe (2002) 'Defining Illegitimate Debt and Linking Its Cancellation to Economic Justice.' Oslo: Norwegian Church Aid.

International Development Association (2003) 'Heavily Indebted Poor Countries (HIPC) Debt Initiative - Statistical Update.' Washington, DC: International Development Association and International Monetary Fund.

'Joint Statement from African NGOs and Trade Unions as the G8 Summit Comes to an End in Evian, France', 3 June 2003.

Kapifimpanga, Opa (2003) 'AFRODAD's Call for a Fair and Transparent Arbitration Court for Debt.' Paper prepared for a workshop on 'Addressing Unsustainable and Illegitimate Debt - Strategic Options for Civil Society', sponsored by KAIROS and the Halifax Initiative, Ottawa, 26 February.

Khalfan, Ashfaq, King, Jeff, and Thomas, Bryan (2002) 'Advancing the Odious Debt Doctrine.' Montreal: Centre for International Sustainable Development Law, McGill University. www.cisdl.org.

Krueger, Anne (2001) 'International Financial Architecture for 2002: A New Approach to Sovereign Debt Restructuring.' Address to National Economists Club Annual Members Dinner, American Enterprise Institute, Washington, DC, 26 November, 2001. www.imf.org.

Krueger, Anne (2002a) A New Approach to Sovereign Debt Restructuring. Washington, DC: International Monetary Fund. Available from www.imf.org.

Krueger, Anne (2002b) 'Sovereign Debt Restructuring and Dispute Resolution.' Address to Bretton Woods Committee Annual Meeting, Washington DC, 6 June.

Lewis, Stephen (2003) 'Lack of Funding for HIV/AIDS "Mass Murder by Complacency"', 8 January. www.africafiles.org.

Longwe, Sara H. (2003) 'Gender Implications of Bank Privatization in Developing Countries.' In 50 Years is Enough, Economic Justice Newsletter, US Network for Global Economic Justice, March/April.

Manoah, Esipisu (2002) 'Lusaka Must Diversify Economy and Privatize.' Business Day (Johannesburg), 22 February.

New Partnership for Africa's Development (NEPAD) (2001) See www.africafiles.org to reference the document as well as extensive commentary and analysis.

Njoroge, Clement (2001) 'Liberalization Throws Women Onto the Streets.' African Church Information Service, September.

Raffer, Kunibert (1992) 'What's Good for the United States Must be Good for the World: Advocating an International Chapter 9 Insolvency.' In From Cancun to Vienna: International Development in a New World. Vienna: Bruno Kreisky Forum for International Development.

Round, Robin (2003) 'Finding Real Solutions to Unsustainable Debt.' Ottawa: Halifax Initiative. Available at www.halifaxinitiative.org.

Ruiz Diaz, Hugo (2003) 'La Dette Argentine: un cas de force majeure.' Bruxelles: Comité pour l'annulation de la dette du Tiers Monde.

Serieux, John (2001) Journeys Just Begun. Ottawa: North-South Institute.

Tagliabue, John and Bumiller, Elisabeth (2003) 'G8 Leaders Talk Tough on Spread of Nuclear Arms.' New York Times, 3 June.

Toussaint, Eric (2003) 'Iraq, War, Debt and the G8.' Sand in the Wheels Newsletter, No. 173. Paris: ATTAC, 30 April. http://attac.org/indexen.

Ugarteche, Oscar y Acosta, Alberto (2003) 'A favor de un tribunal internacional de arbitraje de deuda soberana (TIADS).' Quito and Lima.

World Bank (2002) Global Development Finance. Washington, DC: World Bank.

World Bank (2003) The Heavily Indebted Poor Countries (HIPC) Debt Initiative: An OED Review. Washington, DC: World Bank.

6
The SDRM versus an International Fair and Transparent Arbitration Process

CIDSE-Caritas Internationalis[1]

INTRODUCTION: CATHOLIC VIEWS ON THE ETHICS OF DEBT

CIDSE is a network that brings together fifteen Catholic development organizations from Europe and North America. Caritas Internationalis is a network of 154 Catholic relief, development and social service organizations present in 200 states and territories throughout the world. As Catholic networks, we are inspired by the daily struggles of Christians around the world working for a humanizing transformation of the global economy. We are also guided by a long history of reflection and debate in Catholic social teaching about the choices we can make so that political and economic affairs are shaped in ways which will serve the needs of all peoples. We are particularly concerned with the worldwide challenges of the creation and distribution of wealth in ways which can achieve the urgent eradication of currently intolerable levels of poverty.

This year we celebrate the fortieth anniversary of Pope John XXIII's major encyclical Pacem in terris. We remain convinced of the relevance of its major insights:

1. Political and international affairs and the multiplicity of arrangements which constitute the international economic, social and political order need to be ruled by moral values recognizable by all people.
2. The increasing recognition of human rights, grounded in the dignity of all human beings, offers great hope for a better solution to world crises.
3. There is an urgent need to strive for the creation of international forms of government to ensure the ability of a globalizing world to truly work for the common good.

In developing our critical response to the present proposals of the IMF with regard to the Sovereign Debt Restructuring Mechanism (SDRM), we lean on these insights and their subsequent development. In considering proposals which will affect financial opportunities for millions, we start from the core belief affirmed repeatedly by John Paul II, that the goods of the earth are given by God to 'the whole human race for the sustenance of all its members, without excluding or favouring anyone' (Centesimus annus 31). Catholic teaching does acknowledge the potential positive role of the market in the international economy. However, we are equally aware that leaving the development prospects of nations, and millions of people, at the mercy of international financial markets is to abnegate our moral and ethical responsibilities as nations, as governments and as public officials. Catholic social teaching has always pointed out that real world markets, including labour, trade and financial ones, are dominated by the realities of power. Agreements presented as free contracts, and so as bearing the full consequent obligations between employee and employer, or trading nations, or borrower and lender, are in reality shaped by unequal power relations.

Whatever claims are made in favour of the markets, we recall the fact that 'there are many human needs which find no place on the market'. With John Paul II, we insist that it is 'a strict duty of justice not to allow fundamental human needs to remain unsatisfied, and not to allow those burdened by such needs to perish' (Centesimus annus 34). In the face of the inequality on which international financial markets are founded, Catholic teaching does not passively or fatalistically accept this as the way of the world, but calls on those with power, and especially those with government power, to protect the weaker parties to such contracts. As we become more and more conscious of the extent and the limits of globalization, we stress 'that it is the universal common good which demands that control mechanisms should accompany the inherent logic of the market' (John Paul II, Address to Pontifical Academy of Social Sciences, 2001). Ensuring that there are such control mechanisms to serve the common good is the responsibility of governments.

Over the last few years the Catholic Church has followed carefully the debates about international debt. While recognizing the principle that debts should be paid, the teaching places very clear limits on the extent of this obligation. For us, in the face of the continued unwillingness of political leaders to provide a humane solution to the blight caused by international debt, the words of John Paul remain as important as ever: 'It cannot be expected that the debts which have been contracted should be paid at the price of unbearable sacrifices' (Centesimus annus 35). We also believe there can be no human development which does not allow people to be active participants in the key decisions which determine its possibilities. Not to allow for meaningful participation is to deny the basic human dignity of people and poorer nations.

Catholic social teaching does not prescribe detailed answers on specific proposals with regard to economic development. But faced with the major new proposals being made to shape the international community's response to debt problems, it does urge us to ask the following basic questions:

1. Does the proposal move us in the direction of achieving progress in ensuring that the goods of the earth are distributed in a way which respects the basic human rights of all people?
2. Does the proposal allow for effective international government cooperative action to protect the needs of the poor?
3. Does the proposal allow for meaningful participation of those who will be most affected by its measures?

These questions are in accordance with two principles of the Church's social teaching: the principle of subsidiarity – where the decisions that most affect poverty reduction efforts of peoples and whole communities must be most influenced by those peoples and communities; and the principle of the preferential option for the poor – where the economic decisions that affect whole countries must start with a full consideration of their effects on poor people.

Background

The last two decades have seen the economic prospects of many developing countries thwarted by debt crises. Creditors have responded with a series of piecemeal but ultimately unsatisfactory mechanisms. Since the 1980s, various solutions have been proposed by commercial creditors (with the so-called Brady initiative) and sovereign creditors (with various Paris Club arrangements) and, more recently, with the Heavily Indebted Poor Country (HIPC) initiative. The HIPC framework marked the first real attempt to establish a more comprehensive approach to low-income debtor countries.

Most of these initiatives have proved inadequate. Even the more comprehensive HIPC initiative has failed to meet its key objectives – a robust exit from unsustainable debts or a clear integration of poverty reduction goals.

The 1990s also witnessed the growing severity and frequency of debt crises for middle-income countries. These new and more rapid crises have largely arisen from the integration of the capital markets in emerging market economies and the introduction of IMF-recommended capital account liberalizations. The resulting huge inflows of volatile capital – leading to crises in Mexico, Asia, Russia and more recently Argentina – have made it necessary for the IMF to organize increasingly expensive rescue packages. But even these 'rescues' have led to criticism of the IMF for bailing out private lenders with public money at the expense of the longer-term development prospects of millions of people.

While the new debt crises in middle-income countries have led to increasing costs, debt-restructuring packages have become more complicated. There is now a greater diversity of creditors (including banks, bond holders and trade financiers) involved in restructuring exercises. Debt restructuring packages that require collective action and coordination between creditors and debtors have become more difficult to achieve. According to the IMF, 'the present process for restructuring … is more prolonged, more unpredictable and more damaging to the country and its creditors than would be desirable.' Moreover, the absence of a 'predictable and equitable process … makes it more difficult to attract long-term capital to the emerging market asset class' (Anne Krueger, April 2002: 20).

Mounting public sector costs and the complexities associated with private sector bailouts have added to the pressure for a more comprehensive approach and for burden-sharing between creditors, particularly the 'bailing-in' of private sector creditors. This has resulted in the IMF putting forward proposals for a new debt restructuring mechanism where some of the principles of domestic insolvency procedures are applied to sovereign countries.

SDRM

Since November 2001, Anne Krueger, IMF first deputy managing director, has outlined a model of an insolvency mechanism in several speeches and articles.[2] In August 2002 the IMF released 'further considerations' on the SDRM, fleshing out the Fund's proposal in more details. According to the IMF:

- The new objective for a so-called Sovereign Debt Restructuring Mechanism 'is to facilitate the orderly, predictable, and rapid restructuring of unsustainable sovereign debt' (Krueger 4) and to 'bind all creditors to a restructuring agreement that has been accepted by a qualified majority' (Häusler 5).

- SDRM should only be used if the debt burden is 'clearly unsustainable' (Krueger 4) and if there is no other way for a country to come to a restructuring agreement with its creditors.
- SDRM should only be invoked when requested by the debtor country and not by the IMF or other creditors.
- The debtor country cannot request an automatic stay/suspension in its debt repayments. The IMF only suggests a 'hotchpot rule' which should make sure that creditors who recovered amounts through litigation should in the end not be better off than those who do not (Gianviti 9, 35ff.).
- Key decisions about the terms of the restructuring would be in the hands of the debtor and a qualified majority of the creditors, and their agreement would be binding on any dissenting minority of creditors, preventing them from pursuing litigation to full payment.
- To legally bind minority creditors, collective action clauses (CACs) in all international sovereign bonds are needed (Krueger 29). These clauses would limit the scope of debts eligible for restructuring to very recent debts. The IMF therefore proposes as a complementary measure an amendment of the IMF's Articles to 'provide the legal basis to make (the) agreement (between the debtor and its creditors) binding on all relevant creditors' (Häusler 6).
- A 'Sovereign Debt Dispute Resolution Forum' (SDDRF) would be established. The forum is not envisaged as a formal decision-making body, but would only administer claims as well as resolve disputes that may arise during the process (Häusler 26ff.). According to the IMF, the members of this forum would be chosen in a lengthy process, whereas the IMF managing director shall designate a selection panel. This panel identifies a pool of candidates from which 'judges would be empanelled when a crisis arises' (Gianviti 11). The IMF governors approve the list of recommended names. The president of the SDDRF would choose four persons out of the recommended list in the case of an actual SDRM.
- Temporary exchange controls to prevent capital flight during the process would be necessary.
- To provide the necessary flexibility when handling a broad scope of the debt, as well as a broad diversity of instruments and creditors, the IMF proposes to organize creditors into different classes, each of which would have to agree to the proposed arrangement with at least 75 per cent of outstanding claims in each class.
- Domestic debts could be included (as a separate class), but decisions regarding these debts should be made on a case-by-case basis. If much of this debt is held by the banking system, 'differential treatment … would need to be accommodated under either approach' (Häusler 17). The board of the IMF favoured a solution in which domestic debts 'should be excluded from the SDRM, at least initially'.

- There is a question as to whether bilateral official debts would be included in any SDRM negotiation (Krueger 18). According to the IMF, both options are possible: the Paris Club could stay outside the SDRM (though close coordination is necessary) or it could be included in the mechanism, but as a separate class (Häusler 21ff.). IMF staff tends to exclusion (Gianviti 25), whereas the private sector prefers inclusion (Gianviti 23).
- Although SDRM purports to support 'creditor equity' (Krueger 9) and creditor burden-sharing, the claims for repayments to be made to the IMF and other multilaterals would still have priority and would be exempt from consideration under SDRM. 'These claims would not be subject to the mechanism' (Krueger 17).
- During an SDRM and a stay on the repayment of creditors, the debtor will still need new money. New debts incurred in this period should be 'senior to all pre-existing private indebtedness' (Krueger 17; emphasis added). Such priority financing 'could also finance payments to priority creditors'.
- To protect the hierarchy of creditor interests, the debtor country is not explicitly required to suspend payments to non-priority creditors during an SDRM ('hotchpot rule').
- The IMF is explicit in its proposal that the debtor country has to follow an 'IMF-supported programme' or is 'working closely with the IMF to elaborate policies' (Krueger 16).
- Decisions are to be made by the majority of creditors in direct negotiations with the debtor.
- The crucial question of who should assess debt sustainability is left open: 'whether it is necessary to provide an independent confirmation of the member's representation of unsustainability as a condition for activation and, if so, who should perform this function' (Gianviti 27).
- The IMF would maintain an important role when assessing the debtor country's economic policy (Gianviti 25), as well as in the approval of the list of candidates for SDDRF (Gianviti 61).

The IMF acknowledges that a 'more orderly framework for debt restructuring will provide investors greater incentives to differentiate between risks' (Krueger, November 2002). Krueger even predicts that 'over time (there should be) a reduction in the borrowing costs for the asset class as a whole.'

An assessment of SDRM

CIDSE and Caritas Internationalis welcome the new IMF initiative, which accepts some of the principles of domestic insolvency procedures. We believe that the IMF's SDRM proposal includes a number of positive elements:

- It marks an acknowledgement that a new debt resolution mechanism could reduce restructuring costs for debtors and creditors alike.
- It would speed up the resolution of a country's indebtedness. Moreover, because there would be an end to lengthy debt rescheduling negotiations,

countries would avoid falling into deeper arrears and thus be spared the costs of having to pay back capitalized interest.

- The proposal has the potential to introduce new disciplinary pressures on creditor lending behaviour.
- It recognizes that during the restructuring process, new loans are needed.
- It would establish a predictable process that produces binding decisions on creditors and debtors and overcomes current difficulties.

Nevertheless, CIDSE and Caritas Internationalis find that many features of the IMF's proposal would retain or reinforce many of the inequities in existing processes. In direct opposition to what we believe to be a key role of governing organizations, we see no attempt in the proposal by those responsible for governing in the interests of the common good, to actually address the core problem of unequal relationships between debtors and creditors. In particular, CIDSE/CI oppose the following IMF proposals:

- The SDDRF is not a decision-making body, but has solely administrative tasks. It would operate at arm's length from the IMF. There are fears that, due to the proposed voting mechanism, the most powerful IMF members (i.e. the G7) will have a disproportionate influence in selecting SDDRF members. It is therefore hard to see how the forum could live up to its four main principles (as set out by Anne Krueger): 'independence, competence, diversity and impartiality.'
- The SDRM mechanism would focus on private sector creditors and therefore mainly emerging markets. This move would in effect create two classes of debtor countries: those with or without significant debt owed to private sector creditors.
- SDRM is not comprehensive. Multilateral debt is excluded, even though the proposal purports to promote the concept of 'creditor equity'. Despite its shortcomings, the HIPC initiative has proven that multilateral debt can be included in equitable frameworks among creditors. Furthermore, it is still not clear if official bilateral (Paris Club and non-Paris Club) debt is to be included in the mechanism and therefore whether the principle of equal burden sharing among all creditor classes is being eroded further.
- The IMF has a pivotal role in selecting the members of the Resolution Forum, while (at least indirectly) also defining the conditionalities to which a debtor country must submit in order to be able to qualify for restructuring.

The IMF is right when it asserts: 'An important goal is to create as clear and predictable framework as possible … debtors and creditors will know what to expect, encouraging them to reach agreement voluntarily "in the shadow of the law."' What Krueger overlooks is that, contrary to the ethical principles that governments around the world give legal force to in establishing domestic bankruptcy regimes, and that give effect to our basic concern that governments offer legal protection to the weaker parties in contracts, SDRM provides no institution or judge that would compel debtor and creditors to negotiate, as the SDDRF has no decision-making role.

Moreover, the Fund's proposal is highly deficient when it attempts to establish a debt restructuring mechanism that is based on the principles of transparency and equity. It does not explicitly consider the impact of debt on the poorest sectors of the country's population, and how any solution would address their needs and interests; nor does it even consider the crucially important issue of participation of stakeholders (i.e. the debtor country's population) and the transparency of the whole process.

A fair and transparent arbitration procedure

CIDSE and Caritas Internationalis agencies work in over 198 countries and territories.[3] Together with our partners working in development and relief, we have direct experience of coping with the effects of national indebtedness on impoverished communities and peoples. We hold strongly to the belief that the purpose of economic systems and structures is to serve the needs of all peoples. To this end, we believe that the current debate over recasting international debt management mechanisms must put the interests of poverty reduction and impoverished people at its centre. While the status quo and much of the IMF's current thinking gives centrality to the interests of creditors (including multilateral institutions), we believe that the proper role for instruments aimed at resolving debt crises can only work with widespread approval when they meet the basic minimum demands our tradition of Catholic social teaching sets before us. A mechanism with a one-sided emphasis on the rights of creditors – private and public – while ignoring those most vulnerable to what the mechanism does cannot meet these demands.

As international development and advocacy agencies that focus on the consequences of debt crises for the poorest and most vulnerable people, CIDSE and Caritas Internationalis have long advocated an alternative debt restructuring mechanism that would be a fair and transparent procedure for fair and equal relationships between debtors and creditors. An 'international procedure' where 'neutral courts of arbitration' are established is a mechanism championed by our networks as a way of providing a durable solution to this problem.

Therefore, CIDSE and Caritas Internationalis propose a debt restructuring mechanism that would modify the proposed fair and transparent arbitration procedure promoted by many non-governmental organizations in North and South.

We believe there is an opportunity to create a mechanism which will come closer to delivering on supporting effective poverty reduction, will express governments' commitment to protection of the vulnerable, and would allow the genuine integrity of the mechanism to be checked through ensuring adequate participation of those whose lives will be most seriously affected by it. And so the key features of the mechanism should be as follows:

- The process shall be open to all debtor countries, including HIPCs.
- The start of the process shall automatically trigger a standstill on all external debt repayments. This would protect countries from litigation by creditors such as 'vulture funds'.

- The debtor and the creditors alike shall choose the members of an independent arbitration panel that could be established in an ad hoc manner. If a more permanent independent body is envisaged to deal with successive debt crises, it could be institutionalized within a structure such as the United Nations, given its special responsibility for the follow-up to the Financing for Development process.
- Debt sustainability shall be judged by this independent panel. It would ensure considerations of debt sustainability within the development context of each debtor country, whereby government revenues are balanced against the needs to finance poverty reduction programmes.
- Similarly, creditors and debtors would reach a specific agreement for using the debt savings in part to benefit the poorest and most vulnerable sectors of the population. The independent panel would judge the adequacy of this agreement.
- The population of the debtor country, through its representatives (parliament, chambers of commerce, trade unions, grassroots organizations, churches, NGOs, etc.) shall have a right to be heard before the panel and will assess the balance of interests between the creditors, the priority need to finance poverty reduction programmes, as well as the debtor country's medium to long-term economic interests.
- The role of the IMF shall be restricted to that of a lender. It may act as a consultant on behalf of all or some creditors, if they so wish. But the IMF cannot act in any 'independent' role because of its creditor function.
- The whole process, including the decisions of the panel, shall be made public.

Notes

1 This chapter is a background paper. The analysis and proposals presented do not necessarily reflect the views of all CIDSE and Caritas Internationalis members. The first draft was written by Martina Newrith/KOO and includes contributions from members of the CIDSE/CI Task Group on Debt and Structural Adjustment (GH3). The CST part was written by Seamus O'Gorman IJND.

2 This section refers mainly to Krueger, Anne (April 2002) – referred to as 'Krueger'; Häusler, Gerd/Gianvitis, Francois/Geithner, Timothy (August 2002), IMF Paper – referred to as 'Häusler'; and Gianviti, F./Geithner, T. (November 2002), IMF Paper – referred to as 'Gianviti.

3 This section is partly based on the research of Kunibert Raffer (University of Vienna), who has been working on this issue for the past 15 years, and Jürgen Kaiser (Erlassjahr.de, Germany).

References

Boorman, Jack (2002) 'Towards a Fair and Orderly Resolution of debt Crises.' Speaking Note, CIDSE Conference, 26 September 26.

Boorman, Jack (2002) 'Sovereign Debt Restructuring: Where Stands the Debate?' http://www.imf.org/external/np/speeches/2002/101702.htm.

CIDSE and Caritas Internationalis (1998) 'Putting Life Before Debt.' http://www.cidse.org/pubs/finaldebteng.html.

CIDSE and Caritas Internationalis (2001) 'Statement on Debt.' http://www.cidse.org/pubs/briefdeb.htm.

Fritz, T. and Hersel, P. (2002) Fair and Transparent Arbitration Processes: A New Road to Resolve Debt Crisis. Berlin: FDCL-Verlag.

Gianviti, François and Geithner, Timothy (2002) The Design of the Sovereign Debt Restructuring Mechanism – Further Considerations.' IMF Paper, November.

Häusler, Gerd, Gianvitis, François, and Geithner, Timothy (2002) 'Sovereign Debt Restructuring Mechanism – Further Considerations.' IMF Paper, August.

IMF (2002) 'IMF Board Discusses Possible Features of a New Sovereign Debt Restructuring Mechanism.' Public Information Notice (PIN) No. 02/106, September.

John Paul II (2001) Address to the participants of seventh plenary session of the Pontifical Academy of Social Sciences, April, par. 2. http://www.vatican.va/roman_curia/pontifical_academies/acdscien/documents/acta7-1of3.pdf.

CIDSE-Caritas Internationalis (2001) Human Development Approach to Debt Sustainability Analyses.

CIDSE-Caritas Internationalis (2003) CIDSE/Caritas Internationalis Background Paper, April: 9.

Kaiser, Jürgen (February 2002) 'Zum dritten Statement von Anne Krueger.' www.erlassjahr.de/15_publikationen/15_ftap020207_ej_krueger_3.htm.

Kaiser, Jürgen (June 2002) 'Der IWF lässt die Maske fallen.' http://www.erlassjahr.de/15_publikationen/15_ftap020630_iwf_maske.htm.

Kaiser, Jürgen (November 2002) 'Firmly on the Wrong Path: SDRM after the Annual Meetings 2002.' http://www.erlassjahr.de/15_publikationen/15_ftap021129_firmly.htm.

Krueger, Anne (November 2001) 'International Financial Architecture for 2002: A New Approach to Sovereign Debt Restructuring.' www.imf.org/external/np/speeches/2001/112601.htm.

Krueger, Anne (December 2001) 'A New Approach to Sovereign Debt Restructuring.' www.imf.org/external/np/speeches/2001/122001.htm.

Krueger, Anne (January 2002) 'The Evolution of Emerging Market Capital Flows: Why We Need to Look Again at Sovereign Debt Restructuring.' www.imf.org/external/np/speeches/2002/012102.htm.

Krueger, Anne (April 2002) 'A New Approach to Sovereign Debt Restructuring.' www.imf.org/external/pubs/cat/longres.cfm?sk=15722.0.

Krueger, Anne (July 2002) 'Preventing and Resolving Financial Crisis: The Role of Sovereign Debt Restructuring.' www.imf.org/external/np/speeches/2002/072602.htm.

Krueger, Anne (September 2002) 'Statement on Sovereign Debt Restructuring Mechanism – Further Considerations.' http://www.imf.org/external/np/pdr/sdrm/2002/090402.htm.

Krueger, Anne (October 2002) 'Crisis Prevention and Resolution: The Role of Sovereign Debt Restructuring.' http://www.imf.org/external/np/speeches/2002/100702a.htm.

Krueger, Anne (November 2002) 'Sovereign Debt Restructuring Mechanism: One Year Later.' http://www.imf.org/external/np/speeches/2002/111202.htm.

Paulus, Christoph G. (2002) A Legal Order for Insolvencies of States.' Unpublished paper.

Raffer, Kunibert (January 2002) 'The Final Demise of Unfair Debtor Discrimination? – Comments on Ms Krueger's Speeches.' http://mailbox.univie.ac.at/~rafferk5.

Raffer, Kunibert (2002) 'Solving Sovereign Debt Overhang by Internationalizing Chapter 9 Procedures.' In Studien von Zeitfragen, 36. Jahrgang, http://www.studien-von-zeitfragen.net/Weltfinanz/RAFFER_1/raffer_1.HTM.

7

Advancing the Odious Debt Doctrine

Jeff King, Ashfaq Khalfan and Bryan Thomas

Part 1: Advancing the Odious Debt Doctrine

INTRODUCTION

This chapter is concerned with three distinct projects: (1) defining the 'odious debt' doctrine as it has been presented in the literature thus far; (2) examining the support for the doctrine under international law; and (3) examining problematic aspects of applying the doctrine under legal settings, and proposed solutions thereto.

The odious debt claim involves two assertions: (1) a definitional claim that odious debts exist under certain conditions, and (2) a legal claim that odious debts are not enforceable against the alleged debtor state under international law.

DEFINITION OF ODIOUS DEBT

As we are concerned with making a legal argument, the very definition of the doctrine is tailored to suit the requirements of a judicially enforceable claim. The activist may well want to adopt a less restrictive definition, but would be advised to keep the comprehensive one offered when considering legal avenues. In defining the doctrine, all of the relevant accessible legal literature on the doctrine has been read and relevant comments synthesized, such that the views of each of the authors are taken into account. Therefore, the definition is not new, but rather a synthesis of existing 'legally recognizable' opinions. 'Legally recognizable' means that the sources are the kinds that may be cited before tribunals. There is an informal hierarchy of such sources, which roughly amounts to (1) treaties, (2) state practice, (3) judicial decisions, (4) writings of recognized publicists, namely, those writing recognized legal texts or in recognized academic journals, and (5) the general principles of law common to many nations. That investigation yields the following conclusion:

> Odious debts are those contracted against the interests of the population of a state, without its consent and with the full awareness of the creditor.

This requires three conditions:

1. Absence of consent: The population must not have consented to the transaction in question. This is so because it is unlikely that the law would forbid a person from willingly entering into a contract that is detrimental to him or her. With dictatorial regimes this requirement presents few problems, while with democratic ones it could pose one.
2. Absence of benefit: According to the applicable writings, there must be absence of benefit to the population in two ways: (1) in the purpose of the

transaction and (2) in fact. The purpose requirement refers to the fact that creditors should not be punished for good faith loans that were misspent by corrupt governments, and the fact requirement refers to the principle that populations that benefit in fact from bad faith loans are still required to repay them (unjust enrichment).

3. Creditor awareness: This requirement stipulates that the creditor must be aware of the absence of consent and benefit. There are several standards that may be employed for measuring 'awareness' and luckily domestic law provides a sufficiently broad definition of awareness to capture those creditors that shut their eyes to the obvious.

Types of odious debts

Three types of odious debts have been identified by the authors:

1. Hostile debts: debts that are actively aggressive against the interests of a population (e.g. conquest, colonization, war, suppressing secessionist attempts).
2. War debts: debts contracted by a state for the purpose of funding a war, which it eventually loses. The victor is not considered obliged to repay.
3. Third-world debts not in the interests of the population: This title refers to the new category of debts that were neither hostile nor war debts, but were simply harmful burdens assumed by a state but for which the population received no benefit. It is this category with which we are primarily concerned.

EVIDENCE UNDER INTERNATIONAL LAW

Type of claim

The first point to note is that one should not claim that odious debts are illegal under international law. Such a claim would imply that states are legally bound to annul these debts, and that those governments that repaid them in the past were breaking the law when doing so. Rather, one should argue that odious debts are unenforceable under international law. That is, the doctrine of odious debt carves out a qualification to the generally accepted rule of repayment. It is in the form of the following statement: 'If the government had contracted a debt under the following conditions, then it is not obliged to repay it.' Legal shorthand for this is that the debt is unenforceable under international law. Practically, this means trying to show that in cases of odious debts, there is no settled international law requiring repayment.

Categories of recognized sources of international law

International law recognizes the following sources:

Treaties

There is little support for the doctrine under treaties. The doctrine was considered for inclusion in an important convention on state succession (i.e. when a state's sovereignty is passed from one entity/government to another), but was ultimately rejected. This is a double-edged sword: on the one hand, it shows that the doctrine was accepted widely enough to make it into a draft, while on the other it was determinedly struck from the final convention. Another problem is that the adopted convention was itself highly unpopular, and still does not have the number of ratifications required to bring it into force.

Customary international law

It is important to note that, as well as eleven examples in which state practice seems to support directly or indirectly the doctrine of odious debts (see below), there are at least two further examples, namely, the Ethiopian and Iranian cases of debt repudiation. The latter is a particularly direct contemporary application of the doctrine, and would probably be well supportive of the doctrine. Not all of the examples are without difficulties, however. In order to evaluate their weight as evidence, it will be necessary to consult international lawyers with extensive experience in litigation. Another issue dealt with under this category is the question of whether states that have repaid their 'odious debts' did so because they felt obliged by law, or rather because they were too concerned about the fallout of not doing so. If it were the latter, then the opinio juris would not accompany repayment and the existence of a settled rule of repayment in those cases can be challenged.

General principles of law

Unjust enrichment is the claim that one cannot receive a benefit at another's expense without conferring a reciprocal benefit. The doctrine of abuse of rights stipulates that one cannot exercise one's rights in an excessive and unreasonable manner, such that it harms the rights of another. Both doctrines have a settled history in domestic law and international law, but the extent to which they are applicable to cases of odious debts may be questioned. I suggest that they are better viewed as supplementary arguments upon which less emphasis should be placed. (It is implicit in this claim that a tribunal may find it quite far-fetched to try to justify the odious debts doctrine on these bases.)

Another argument that is far more convincing, however, is the law of domestic agency. Domestic law contains provisions that govern the way in which one person can create legal obligations for another. This arrangement is similar in international law, where the government creates legally binding obligations for the state, the latter of which includes its population. Agency law is useful in that the very power of making binding commitments for another is considered to carry with it the special responsibility of acting in the interests of that person. This is known as a fiduciary obligation under the common law, and has its equivalent under the civil law. A fiduciary obligation is an obligation that exists when one person has the legal obligation to act for the benefit of another. Classic relationships include doctors and patients, lawyers and clients, corporations and shareholders and principals and agents. Even more promising in this respect is that under domestic law, a third party can be held liable for assisting an agent in the breach of their obligations toward their principal. So if a bank were to knowingly assist an executive defraud a corporation, that bank can be held liable for the losses of the principal. The law requires that the third party 'know' of the breach of obligation, and thus defines 'knowledge' for this purpose. This definition includes actual awareness and wilfully shutting one's eyes to the obvious. This domestic law analogy is probably the single most convincing argument in favour of odious debt that we have yet come across.

PROBLEMATIC ASPECTS AND PROPOSED SOLUTIONS

Here I attempt to pre-empt what I view as the chief arguments that will be offered in response to the legal claim. The opponent may argue that even if the foregoing were true, the doctrine would be impossible to apply in practice because of problems assessing consent, benefit and awareness, and because of the cardinal importance of the difference between state succession and government succession. The conclusions may be summarized briefly as follows.

Absence of consent

Once the absence of benefit to the population has been proved, the burden shifts to the creditor to prove that there was in fact consent to the transaction in question.

Absence of benefit

Purpose

Five categories of loans for specific 'odious' reasons are given. In cases where the loans are for no particular reason at all, the question turns to the nature of the regime. Where it is dictatorial or quasi-dictatorial, it is presumptively without benefit to the population. Where democratic or quasi-democratic, the reverse presumption operates.

Fact

The debtor state bears the burden for establishing absence of benefit.

Four categories of disbursements are given as prima facie cases of spending that is not in the interests of the population. Where the loaned funds were applied to general government revenue, the government budgets for the respective years must be classified according to spending on (1) oppressive, (2) neutral and (3) beneficial institutions. The issues of the indeterminacy of this procedure and absence of governmental records are addressed.

Creditor awareness

Three standards are borrowed from the common law of Canada and the United Kingdom:

(1) actual knowledge;

(2) wilfully shutting one's eyes to the obvious; and

(3) wilfully and recklessly failing to make such inquiries as an honest and reasonable person would make.

Part 2: Sites and Strategic Legal Options for Addressing Illegitimate Debt

INTRODUCTION

This chapter is meant to define and support the odious debts doctrine in a sufficiently legal way, and will likely be a better reference paper than an inspiring description of the doctrine. Analysis indicates that the doctrine of odious debt can be clearly defined, has a fair bit of support under the traditional categories of international law, and can be modified to withstand prima facie theoretical objections. The results are almost surprising. Upon hearing of the doctrine, anyone familiar with public international law is likely to be virtually certain that the doctrine could never be applied in practice. However, after examining the state practice, general principles of law and writings and judicial decisions, it seems that there is much more material available to make such an argument than one would initially think. If nothing else, there are legally persuasive arguments in favour of the morally compelling doctrine of odious debt.

There are various legal avenues open to civil society organizations (CSOs) and southern states for advancing the odious debt campaign and the campaign against debts that violate economic and social rights. The value of each of these approaches will be assessed. One should note at the outset that one must separately address the debts of southern states owed to other states, to international financial institutions (IFIs) and to private banks located in other countries. Each of these categories of creditors raises different issues in relation to the possibilities for redress.

The rest of this chapter will analyse the relationship of political efforts and their relationship to legal approaches. It then examines a variety of judicial approaches to address odious debt issues. Finally, it addresses the utility of addressing illegitimate debt through the prism of economic and social rights and of using the UN Committee on Economic, Social and Cultural Rights (CESR).

POLITICAL APPROACHES

It is theoretically possible for debtor states unilaterally and collectively to cancel illegitimate debts. The main obstacle to such action is the ability of creditor states and organizations to suspend foreign aid and lending. This danger may be mitigated in two ways. First, the assessment of odious and other illegitimate debt must be seen to be fair and to follow consistent principles. Second, it is necessary that there be a high degree of international acceptance of the odious debt doctrine among most southern states and at least some northern states.

It is suggested that the decision of an influential judicial body in favour of the odious debt doctrine may have influence beyond its jurisdiction so as to legitimize the general application of the doctrine. Such a decision could have a significant effect on the bargaining dynamic between creditor and debtor states, possibly leading to debt write-downs. In addition, by increasing the prospect of further repudiations, it could create an incentive for the creation of an international tribunal to assess illegitimate debt claims. Finally, by setting out the parameters of acceptable policy, such a decision would facilitate efforts by southern states to develop common stances on this issue.

Civil society groups may play a role in generating and popularizing principles that influence the understanding and development of international law. An example can be taken from the civil society effort to declare the use or threat of use of nuclear weapons as illegal, using popular tribunals, mass mobilization and eventually taking the case to the International Court of Justice.

JUDICIAL APPROACHES

There are many possible sites for litigation. This situation should be seen as an opportunity for advocates of debt cancellation. It is necessary to identify the best venues in which to create precedents that will lead to the resolution of disputes in political fora and potentially to stimulate the creation of an international tribunal on this issue. In selecting the first test case(s), the following should be considered:

1. The possible risks involved in terms of economic retaliation against the plaintiff and the effect of a negative decision.
2. The procedural rules which limit certain disputes to certain fora.
3. The extent to which a particular jurisdiction will be favourable to the odious debt doctrine.

The dispute resolution body that may be approached in relation to a particular dispute will depend on the nature of the lender – whether it is a state, an IFI or a private institution – and also on whether the loan agreement includes a choice of forum clause (such clauses attempt to specify which court can decide this issue).

An important related issue will be which body of law will be applied – this may be international law or the domestic law of any state. This issue is important since there is more known support for the doctrine in international law than in domestic law. However, some doctrines that are common to most domestic laws show promise in supporting the odious debts doctrine. There is therefore a significant need for more research on the treatment of odious debt by the domestic laws of a number of key states.

The International Court of Justice

The ICJ may be used where the lender is a state and where the loan contract does not specify any particular forum (which is the norm in state to state contracts). The ICJ is probably the ideal eventual forum: its judges are relatively independent of any one state and more likely to be open to non-traditional arguments. Its decision would be extremely influential; although ICJ judgements do not create law to the same extent as customary international law and treaties, they are a subsidiary source of international law and are seen in some instances as authoritative evidence of the law.

Another advantage of the ICJ is that it can provide an Advisory Opinion. This decision would not be binding in itself, but would provide legitimacy to the odious debt doctrine, thereby allowing it to be applied to individual situations. An Advisory Opinion can be framed in general terms, thereby entailing less risk on the part of any one debtor state and allowing the court to address the validity of the doctrine itself, rather than any one particular dispute.

Recourse to the court is limited. The states involved must normally consent to the ICJ jurisdiction. The exceptions are where all the states before the court have accepted in advance the 'compulsory jurisdiction' of the ICJ, or where a treaty between them specifies recourse to the ICJ. Here are four strategic options that civil society can attempt to utilize (not in order of preference).

'Sweetheart' litigation
A creditor state, whether developed or developing, could be approached to allow a case to proceed against it, so as to set a precedent. This is most realistic in situations where the debts were lent by a previous regime within the creditor state (loans by states such as South Africa or Brazil would be appropriate where these have not yet been cancelled). However, this option on its own may affect the international credit rating of the debtor. This approach may be combined with the joint suit option, below.

Advisory opinion requested by General Assembly
This is probably the most desirable option. However, it would require the support of a majority of states in the General Assembly (UNGA), who choose to vote on the issue. This would require the active support of roughly sixty states. The campaign against nuclear weapons succeeded in gaining such a UNGA request, mainly by cultivating certain key states as allies and by originally raising the issue within a political body that was insulated from the diplomatic pressure of nuclear states.

The debt cancellation movement should consider using bodies such as the Non-Aligned Movement and the G77 for this purpose. Although many southern governments will not be comfortable about the conditionality that necessarily accompanies the odious debt doctrine, this may be mitigated by emphasizing the doctrine's potential application to the apartheid debts of South Africa.

Advisory opinion requested by UN agency
UN bodies such as the FAO, ILO, WHO, UNESCO, the World Bank and IMF and ECOSOC have the ability to request an advisory opinion. By virtue of their institutional ethos, some bodies may be more willing than the General Assembly to make a request. It should be noted, however, that the UNDP and UNCTAD are not empowered to make such a request. However, the ICJ will only entertain such a request if it determines that the issue falls within the scope of the agency's duties. The World Health Organization's request to the ICJ for an Advisory Opinion on the legality of nuclear weapons was rejected on this basis. However, it must be noted that the commencement of the campaign in the WHO created a momentum that convinced the General Assembly to make a successful request to the ICJ.

Joint suit by a group of states against one creditor state
This approach has the advantage of minimizing the risk taken by any one state. However, with a large number of states, each of the parties will need to have recognized the compulsory jurisdiction of the ICJ. Failing this, the consent of the creditor to the case is required. This will normally only be possible in a hostile

context if some of the debtor states are large middle-income countries that can make credible threats of repudiation.

Barring unusual circumstances, only states can be parties to an ICJ case. ICJ cases will be judged under international law. A small proportion of inter-state loan contracts may specify that the case will be decided under the laws of a domestic state.

It is an open question as to whether the odious nature of a contract allows a choice of law (or a choice of forum) clause in a contract to be struck down. Such situations are best avoided in the first test cases.

Arbitration

This type of dispute resolution will be the norm in contracts with IFIs. It is also possible in contracts with states or private bodies.

Arbitration always rests on the consent of both parties, expressed in the contract or at the time of the dispute. The advantage of such tribunals is that they are faster, are less public (thereby reducing somewhat the exposure of the debtor to retaliation) and are low risk – that is to say, a negative judgement rendered here would not be as much of a setback as a negative ICJ judgement. An arbitral venue may be used so as to indicate a way forward and to shed light on useful arguments for a future case.

The disadvantage is that both parties have more control over the choice of the arbitrators. This is less important for World Bank contracts where each party names one arbitrator, and these two arbitrators select the third arbitrator. In the absence of consensus, the third member of the court is nominated by the president of the ICJ, or the UN secretary general. The creditor therefore cannot screen out certain arbitrators from the tribunal.

Arbitration tribunals are less likely than the ICJ to adopt non-status quo decisions, but more likely do so than domestic courts, since loan contracts do not normally provide for appeals to arbitration. The law that is applied in arbitration is normally international law, where there is no choice of law clause specifying a domestic law.

Domestic courts

The domestic courts and the laws of creditor states are selected in the majority of contracts with southern debtors. New York and England are the most common jurisdictions selected. Some loan contracts may specify litigation within the debtor state. However, the ratification of a debt repudiation within such a court is unlikely to carry much weight among creditor nations and is best avoided. Nevertheless, debt litigation within debtor states, such as seen in 2000 in Argentina, may be useful for the purpose of identifying odious debt and putting pressure on a state to take action on it. The primary question for debtor states with odious debts is to determine what the likely decision of the courts of that jurisdiction is likely to be. This should include a determination of what the domestic law's treatment of odious debt is likely to be. The extent to which international law is incorporated into the domestic law is relevant. Jurisdictions such as the US and UK are less open to such incorporation than nations such as Italy. Should a court recognize odious debt doctrines, some states can legislate to exclude such determinations. The general attitude of the courts of a jurisdiction should also be considered. New York case law, for example, indicates that the courts self-consciously refer to the importance of maintaining New York as a centre of lending and that this requires them to safeguard the sanctity of contracts.

It may be possible for a debtor state to avoid its case being heard in an inhospitable forum in spite of a choice of forum and law clause. In order to do this, it will have to find another forum that has a reasonable relationship to the contract and which is willing to overturn the terms of the contract either on public policy grounds, the fraud of the creditor, or on the basis that the choice of forum or law clause in an odious loan is itself 'odious'. Some jurisdictions, such as England, will refuse to hear cases where England was chosen as jurisdiction so as to avoid mandatory rules of public order in another forum. However, it should be noted that such defences are exceptional.

Another possibility is for a debtor state to assert doctrines of sovereign immunity, act of state and comity, all of which refer to the principle that courts of one state cannot judge the acts of another state. In the US, and in most northern states, such doctrines are often not interpreted to apply to loan contracts, which are seen as commercial rather than state acts. However, sovereign immunity is relevant at the time of seizure of assets. It would not be advisable for a debtor state to rely on these defences on their own, since this would harm international confidence in its ability to meet its legal commitments. However, such defences may be used so as to force the dispute to a more neutral forum, including international tribunals.

CSOs have a major role to play in using the courts of debtor states to force debtor governments into action, including as litigants where the procedural rules permit. They may also mobilize support and resources for cases internationally and in creditor states. They may be able to submit amicus curiae briefs to such courts. However, on procedural grounds, it is unlikely that they themselves will be able to bring such cases to international and creditor courts.

TREATY MONITORING BODIES: THE COMMITTEE ON ECONOMIC, SOCIAL AND CULTURAL RIGHTS

The Committee on Economic, Social and Cultural Rights (CESCR) asks for a report from states that are party to the International Covenant on Economic, Social and Cultural Rights (ICESCR) every five years on the measures that they have taken to implement the Covenant. CESCR has tended actively to solicit parallel reports from CSOs from the country in question and to hear their oral opinions. It would be useful for the debt relief movement to engage this process and make representations indicating whether a lender country's debt collection policies for specific countries undermines or reverses progress towards the realization of economic, social and cultural rights in such debtor countries. Such efforts would assist in the collection of useful data on this issue and it can be expected that the report of CESCR will receive significant coverage in the media.

CESCR has previously commented on the possible need for debt relief initiatives so as to protect economic, social and cultural rights in developing states.

The Covenant lays an obligation on states to engage in international cooperation to the maximum of their available resources. This does not necessarily translate into a concrete obligation to give aid. However, in certain circumstances, it may be possible to identify an obligation on a creditor to cancel debt where to not do so would necessarily lead to severe setbacks to the realization of basic economic and social rights in a debtor state. If this issue was brought to its attention, CESCR could encourage the state whose performance it is reviewing to cancel certain debts and may even term the failure to do so a violation of the Covenant.

Conclusion

This chapter demonstrates that there exists a large number of strategic options for the debt cancellation movement to pursue a legal approach, in judicial, political and human rights treaty bodies. Careful analysis will be required before selecting any of the judicial fora. For a large number of debts, this choice will be limited for procedural reasons and due to the terms of the contract. However, this is of lesser concern given that positive determinations on odious debt are only required in some of these fora in relation to some contracts. Once the odious debt doctrine has greater legitimacy and acceptance, there are likely to be more negotiated settlements and possibly a specialized international tribunal.

The odious debt and economic and social rights approaches must be seen as parallel, but complementary, since they have different justifications, often address different debts and will have different effects. Both approaches should be pursued simultaneously.

Part 3: The Odious Debt Doctrine and International Public Policy: Assessing the Options

This chapter examines the applicability of the doctrine of odious debts to less developed countries (LDCs) of the 1970s and early 1980s. It is divided into two sections. The first section focuses on private lending from commercial banks; the second section focuses on lending from international financial institutions (IFIs). The chapter has two aims:

1. To examine the doctrine of odious debts from the point of view of international public policy.
2. To provide a preliminary assessment of the viability of applying the doctrine of odious debts to LDC debts from the period 1971–82.

On the first question, it is argued that the doctrine, if made a fixture of international law, might help to avert future debt crises. On the second, it is suggested that attempts to invoke the doctrine will face considerable legal obstacles, which may or may not be surmountable.

Private Lending: Past, Present and Future

Debt crises are nothing new. For centuries, sovereigns have over-borrowed, private lenders have over-loaned, and crises have arisen as a result. What is new, in the modern era, is that lenders are now far better equipped to ensure that their loans are used for legitimate purposes. As such, lenders can now be held to a higher standard of responsibility for their actions. The doctrine of odious debts requires that lenders be subjectively aware of the odious end-uses of their loans. This requirement is more easily met in the modern era than in past centuries.

According to the conventional explanation, the 1970s surge in lending to developing countries was triggered by a dramatic surge in oil prices. OPEC nations deposited their newfound riches into commercial bank accounts, and commercial banks subsequently loaned these funds to developing countries. In time, predictions of developing country economic growth were disappointed and lenders backed out, prompting the 1982 debt crisis. This explanation is controversial, however. Commercial banks drastically over-extended themselves throughout this period.

Often, it seems, commercial banks turned a blind eye to obvious corruption. Local bank officers (within borrower countries) were held to a low standard of accountability, and so tended to rubber-stamp loans, comfortable that their careers would have advanced by the time any problems arose. Senior bank officials were pleased to extend loans: substantial front-end fees were often paid by lenders, and the value of the loan appeared as an asset on the banks' current balance sheets.

Commercial lenders from this period no doubt expected that their loan contracts were legally enforceable. The doctrine of sovereign immunity – the immunity of states from the jurisdiction of the courts of other states – has steadily eroded over the course of the past century, and moreover, most of the loan contracts from the period in question contained explicit waivers of sovereign immunity. Still, commercial lenders for the most part have chosen not to sue on developing country debt, for fear that doing so would only drive southern states into a bunker mentality, making matters worse for lenders.

There is a serious concern that the doctrine of odious debts, even if successfully invoked to cancel the debt of the 1970s, would cause more problems than it solves. The concern is that any country invoking the doctrine will be punished by international financial markets. However, there is a risk of overstating this point. First, southern countries frequently pay out more to service their debts than they borrow on international financial markets, so they may be wise (from a strictly economic perspective) to simply repudiate their debts unilaterally and endure the 'punishment'. Second, successful invocation of the doctrine of odious debts is not equivalent to unilateral repudiation. Legitimate creditors need only fear the latter. Any attempt to invoke the doctrine of odious debts is seriously complicated by the emergence of debt restructuring agreements and secondary markets for debt. Restructuring agreements were entered into consensually by developing country governments and private lenders. These agreements consolidated outstanding loans, and typically contained cross-default clauses and sharing clauses. Briefly, cross-default clauses stipulate that a default vis-à-vis any single creditor (party to the restructuring agreement) constitutes a default vis-à-vis all creditors. Sharing clauses stipulate that payments made from the debtor to any single creditor be shared (on a pro rata basis) with all creditors. In effect, creditors had their legal interests consolidated by restructuring agreements. Debtors were likewise consolidated by these agreements. Typically, private and public debtors would participate, and a nation's debt would be rolled into one (lengthy) new contract.

Obviously, these restructuring agreements complicate matters from the perspective of the doctrine of odious debts: odious and non-odious debts may now be rolled together. Tracking which loans (of any given country) were odious will be extremely difficult.

Restructuring agreements had the effect of making southern debt fungible: one lender's $100 of debt from, say, Mexico, is worth as much (i.e. involves the same risks) as any other lender's $100 of Mexican debt. As a result, a speculative secondary market in developing country debt emerged in the 1980s. This also complicates things from the point of view of the doctrine of odious debts. It appears that the legal mechanism by which debts are sold on the secondary market may have the effect of extinguishing the original loan contract and creating a new one in its stead. Thus, it may be that those original odious debt contracts from the 1970s are now extinguished, replaced by new (potentially non-odious) ones. This is a complicated legal matter that may present substantial difficulties for those attempting to invoke the doctrine. Where debts have been converted into bonds – which is common – these difficulties become even more substantial.

International Financial Institutions

It is plain that IFIs possess juridical personality, and so may be brought before the courts by countries wanting to invoke the doctrine of odious debts. IFI loan agreements, however, stipulate that disputes be resolved by an international arbitration tribunal.

The World Bank is composed of five sub-groups:

1) International Bank for Reconstruction and Development (IBRD)
2) International Development Agency (IDA)
3) International Finance Corporation (IFC)
4) Multilateral Investment Guarantee Agency (MIGA)
5) International Centre for Investment Dispute Settlement (ICSID)

IBRD is the most important, from the point of view of southern state borrowing. The World Bank is the single largest creditor, accounting for a seventh of developing country debt.

World Bank lending is (and has always been, from a legal perspective) carefully monitored and orchestrated. Nevertheless, World Bank officials, in recent years, have conceded that in the latter part of the twentieth century, officials with the Bank turned a blind eye to corruption. There is little doubt that some portion of developing country debt contracted with the World Bank is odious.

Because World Bank officials were often well aware of the end-uses of their loans, subjective awareness of odious lending may be relatively easy to establish. World Bank officials have, in recent years, essentially confessed that much of the postwar lending was odious. Furthermore, World Bank loans have not been sold on the secondary market, so the forensic problems involved in applying the odious debt doctrine to private lending may be less acute with IFI lending. Indeed, World Bank loans may offer a promising test case for the resurrection of the doctrine of odious debts. Loans from the other major IFI, the IMF, offer a far less promising target for the doctrine of odious debts. IMF loans are intended to serve a strictly macro-economic function (i.e. to correct balance of trade problems) and so IMF officials had less direct involvement in the end uses of loans. Creditors' subjective awareness (of odious end-uses) may therefore be difficult to establish. However, IMF lending forms a far smaller proportion of debt owed to the IFIs.

• Contact details for the autors of this chapter are:
Asfaq Khalfan, Director, akhalfan@cisdl.org
Jeff King, jking@cisdl.org
Bryan Thomas, bthomas@cisdl.org

Centre for International Sustainable Development Law
3661 Peel Street, Montreal, Quebec, Canada H3A 1X1
tel. (1-514), 398-8918; fax (1-514), 398-8197, web-address: www.cisdl.org

8

Odious Iraqi Debt

Eric Toussaint (CADTM)

For twenty years the big powers (who are also the main creditors) have avoided putting the issue of odious debt under the spotlight, while the governments of indebted countries did not contest their odious debt. Then, suddenly, on 10–11 April 2003, the idea of odious debt appeared in the speeches of the Bush administration, demanding that France, Germany and Russia (who had been against the war on Iraq) should drop their claims on Iraq.

The international press seized on the demands and explicitly mentioned odious debt. After a few days, however, most of the press no longer followed up the story, apart from the Financial Times and a few other international papers (International Herald Tribune, Wall Street Journal).

The editorial staff of the Financial Times firmly opposed the idea of renouncing the debt. According to the FT, the same argument would have to be applied to many countries of the developing world and to many former Soviet states. This could give the governments of indebted countries all sorts of ideas – in the end they would wish to have the same thing applied to their own debts. And even if they did not, the social movements in their countries might pick up on the idea (e.g. in Brazil, or in South Africa, where the debt of the apartheid regime has now reached $24 billion). The FT explained that the Bush administration was playing with fire and was putting creditors at risk.

WHAT IS AN ODIOUS DEBT?

If a despotic power [e.g. Saddam Hussein's regime] takes out a loan at odds with the needs and interests of the state in order to strengthen its despotic regime or in order to suppress the population who fights him, this debt is odious for the whole people of that country. This debt involves no obligation to the nation: it's a debt of the regime, a personal debt of the power that took it out, and for this reason it expires with the fall of that same power. (Alexander Sack, Les Effets des transformations des etats sur leurs dettes publiques et autres obligations financières, Recueil Sirey, 1927)

The concept of 'odious' debt is perfectly applicable to Iraq. The doctrine has its origins in the nineteenth century. It was applied during the Spanish–American war in 1898. Cuba, at that time a Spanish colony, was occupied by the USA (as a 'protectorate') and Spain requested the US to pay back the debt owed to it by Cuba. The US refused and declared the debt to be odious; that is, taken out by a despotic regime in order to finance policies at odds with the people's interest. What is important is that this declaration, accepted in the end by Spain, was laid out in an international treaty – the Treaty of Paris – and thus forms a judicial precedent.

Other cases: the debts incurred by Napoleon were renounced during the restoration as 'odious' and contrary to the interests of the French. After the

American Civil War, the victorious North refused to take on the southern debt which had been set for the defence of a slavery-based system. After the First World War, the Treaty of Versailles declared void the debt that the German Kaiser had taken out in order to colonize Poland and stated it could not be transferred to the newly re-established Polish state. The dictatorial regime of Tinoco in Costa Rica ran into debt against the British Crown. Chief Justice Taft of the US Supreme Court, who had been called upon to mediate in the judicial conflict (Great Britain vs. Costa Rica, 1923), decided that the debt was a personal legacy of the despot: the lending bankers shouldn't be going after the democratic regime that followed Tinoco, but at each other, for they had known about the despotic nature of Tinoco's rule. Justice Taft added that the lenders were not able to show that they were trustworthy.

The doctrine of odious debt was first formulated by Alexander Sack (former minister of the Russian Tsar, later professor of law in Paris, having emigrated to France after the revolution of October 1917) in 1927, in his compendium on the transfer of debt in case of regime change. In the following thirty years, no debtor – to our knowledge – made use of the doctrine of odious debt in order unilaterally to renounce a debt or in order to call for mediation.

Jointly with other authors (in particular, Jean-Claude Willame and Patricia Adams) and movements (Jubilee South Africa, Jubilee South), CADTM has long been analysing third world debts from this judicial point of view: the debts incurred by Mobutu (Zaire – Democratic Republic of Congo), by Habyarimana (Rwanda), by Marcos (Philippines), by Suharto (Indonesia), by the Generals of the Argentinean dictatorship, by Pinochet in Chile, by the Uruguayan dictatorship, by the Brazilian dictatorship (in the period 1964–85, the Brazilian debt shot up from \$2.5 billion to \$100 billion – a 40-fold increase during the military rule), the debt of Nigeria, Togo, South Africa, etc.

These are not old stories, since the people of these countries are continuing to pay off these odious debts by taking out more debt. The Democratic Republic of Congo is a case in point: in 2003 the debt amounted to \$13 billion, which corresponded more or less to the total of loans that Mobutu took out, since there has been virtually no new borrowing since he was ousted in 1997. The entire debt of the DRC should thus be dropped.

WHY DID THE BUSH ADMINISTRATION BACK DOWN ON ODIOUS DEBT?

In April 2003 the finance ministers of the G8 nations assembled in Washington, where the secretary of state of the US Treasury, John Snow, demanded that Russia, France and Germany in particular should drop their odious debt towards Iraq. The USA made this demand not because it was interested in seeing the debt dropped, but as a political bargain, as a way of raising the stakes against countries that were opposed to the war. The idea was to find a way to convince France, Germany and Russia to change their position and thereby render legitimate the war. It would also make it possible for those who took military action to start immediately with the reconstruction of Iraq by using its oil revenues without having to service debt payments. The higher the outstanding debt before the war in 2003, the longer the

USA and its allies would have to wait before they could be reimbursed for the costs of reconstruction. Germany responded that dropping the debt was not an issue, and that it would be rescheduled. The USA continued haggling in order to convince France, Russia and Germany to make an effort to drop the debt. In exchange for their good will, companies from their countries could expect to benefit from contracts linked with reconstruction.

Obviously, the USA achieved concessions from the French and Russian side in the end. In fact, on 22 May 2003, the UN Security Council lifted its sanctions against Iraq and charged the US-designated civil administrator in Iraq, namely Paul Bremer, with Iraqi oil exploitation (which had been under UN control). The UN named Sergio Vieira de Mello as its representative in Iraq, with a much lower status compared to Paul Bremer (in August 2003, he was killed in an attack on the UN headquarters in Baghdad, along with 23 others).

Lifting sanctions against Iraq means that companies – above all, US companies – can now do business in Iraq (the Financial Times headlined its story on 23 May 2003: 'UN removal of sanctions clears way for business'). It also means that all the frozen assets of Saddam Hussein and Iraq in general (especially in the USA) for over 12 years are now 'freed up'. As a result, the USA is able to use them for reconstruction: the assets are not recovered by the Iraqi people. The lifting of sanctions by the Security Council 'will free billions of dollars in frozen assets and future oil revenues from UN control and place it at the disposal of coalition forces and interim Iraqi leaders to pay for reconstruction' (Financial Times, 23 May 2003).

SOME HISTORICAL POINTS OF REFERENCE ON THE WAR ON IRAQ

In the 1980s, Saddam Hussein was supported by the USA and its allies in the war against Iran that caused over a million deaths. Iraq incurred debts to the USA and its allies. In 1990, Iraq invaded Kuwait. Several theories exist as to the reasons for this incursion, but it is not impossible that the Bush Snr. administration led Saddam Hussein to believe that such aggression would not elicit any reaction, effectively setting him a trap. After the end of the first war, called Operation Desert Storm by the victors, Saddam Hussein was deliberately kept in power, as the USA feared that the country (and its oil reserves) would otherwise fall into the hands of an uncontrollable revolution in the neighbourhood of Iran, itself uncontrollable. Allied troops allowed Saddam Hussein suppress the uprising in Bassorah. The war was led with a UN mandate, which included the freezing of all Iraqi foreign assets and an embargo.

Later on, the 'oil for food' programme was added. Some 50 per cent of Iraqi oil revenues from this programme were used to buy food and medicine. This was wholly inadequate in the light of the death of more than 500,000 children as a consequence of the embargo. The existence of the programme was widely touted internationally and was even used for propaganda purposes. However, the fact that 25 per cent of the revenues was distributed to neighbouring countries in the form of reparation payments was little known. The United Nations Compensation Commission had, since 1991, recognized the validity of reparation claims totalling \$44 billion (which was only a part of the demands). The claims were filed by individuals, by companies and by governments. With a quarter of all revenues at its disposal, the UNCC handed out – until the war in April 2003 – $17.6 billion to the claimants, prioritizing individuals and families. In terms of reparations, $26 billion worth remain to be paid, while payment has been stalled (Financial Times, 24 June 2003). Absolute priority was not given to the satisfaction of the needs of the Iraqi population – food and medicine – when oil revenues were distributed.

In 2003, a US-led coalition attacked Iraq. Great Britain, Australia, the Netherlands and Denmark directly took part in military action, while other countries provided support in various ways. The coalition acted in violation of the UN Charter, according to which it committed an act of aggression.

IMPOSSIBLE IRAQI DEBT

How high is the Iraqi debt? According to a 2002 study by the Department for Energy of the Bush administration, it probably amounted to $62 billion. According to a joint study of the World Bank and the Bank of International Settlements, it totalled $127 billion, of which $47 billion is in interest payments. According to a private Washington think-tank, the overall level of financial obligations of Iraq (debt, reparations and contractual obligations) was $383 billion at the beginning of 2003, of which $127 billion was estimated as debt.

The creditor countries fall into two categories: members and non-members of the Club of Paris. The Club of Paris includes 19 creditor states and some invited guests (Brazil, Korea), following the fancy of the 19 founders. It estimates that it can claim $21 billion in debts from Iraq, to which $21 billion of due interest payments must be added (Financial Times, 12–13 July, 2003).

The second category of creditors comprises Arab countries (the United Arab Emirates, Kuwait, Egypt, Jordan, Morocco, Saudi Arabia), Turkey and some countries from the former Soviet bloc (Poland, Bulgaria, Hungary), since turned staunch US allies. These countries have a combined claim of about $55 billion in debt. More than half of this sum is claimed by the Gulf states (excluding Kuwait), but this debt is subject to a long-running legal challenge by Iraq. Iraq claims that the $30 billion was a gift from these countries in order to fight the war against Iran, while they insist that the money was a loan.

Together, the two categories of creditor regroup all bilateral debts (in total, $97 billion). The stakes are not as high for the private banks involved. They claim about $2 billion in debts (Bank of New York and JP Morgan being the main creditors). As for the World Bank and the IMF, Iraq's debts to them are below $200 million.

In summary, then, the negotiations between Iraq and its creditors concern, as a starting point of discussion, a sum of around $100 billion: 42 (Club of Paris) + 55 (other bilateral loans) + 2 (banks) + 0.2 (World Bank and IMF) = about 100. This sum does not include outstanding compensation claims (around $160 billion for the 1990–1 war), contracts which were concluded just before the outbreak of war ($90 billion) and above all the new debts incurred since March–April 2003.

In reality, the main negotiation will take place between the creditors themselves and not between creditors and the so-called Iraqi authorities put in place by the USA. The creditors will have to fight over the following question: who will take the lead in renouncing some of the debt so as to make the repayment of the rest of it bearable? 'Bearable' for the creditors here means that the debt can be paid back on the due date. There is no question of the creditors considering whether the repayment of the debt is bearable with respect to the needs of the Iraqi population. The USA will ask its colleagues in the Club of Paris, as well as the Arab countries, Turkey, Poland, Bulgaria and Hungary, to make a joint effort to reduce their claims by a third to two-thirds. If that happens, the amount of bilateral debt could be limited to $65 billion (a one-third reduction) or even $32 billion (two-thirds reduction), instead of the original $97 billion. The USA is keen to achieve such a reduction in order to be able to add to the existing debts those costs arising from reconstruction. Many months of negotiations are therefore to be expected.

In this context, it is worth taking a look at the partition of the debt according to the two opposing factions, which evolved within the Club of Paris before the outbreak of war. At the famous meeting of G7 finance ministers in April 2003 in Washington, it should be remembered, the press noted that Russia, France and Germany were the main creditors of odious debt to Iraq. In reality, the figures are not as clear – as can easily be verified from the table below, where the debt of the War Faction is contrasted to that of the Peace Camp.

Iraqi debt to the Club of Paris (in $ millions)

Peace Camp	War Faction
Russia: 3.450	Japan: 4.100
France: 3.000	USA: 2.200
Germany: 2.400	Italy: 1.720
Canada: 560	Great Britain: 930
Brazil: 200	Australia: 500
Belgium: 180	Spain: 320
	Netherlands: 100
	Denmark: 30
Sum: 9.790	Sum: 9.900

Data source: Financial Times, 12–13 July 2003

This table shows that the War Faction has a greater claim of odious debt than the Peace Camp, which was not the implication of the Bush administration's discourse at the time of its blackmailing attempts in April 2003.

Let us remember that at the start of the negotiations the amount of debt had deliberately been exaggerated. Also, the Club of Paris is claiming for double its due debt: $42,000 million instead of $21,000. How come? Because the Club of Paris adds interest payments on outstanding debt for the period since 1992. This is an absurd demand, since with the sanctions against Iraq, the UN was in control of all the oil revenues. Furthermore, Iraqi assets abroad were frozen. Nevertheless, the Club of Paris has credited the interest (along with most of the other bilateral creditors) and the debt is now doubled. If the demand for interest payments is dropped during the course of the talks, the Club of Paris will present the reduction in debt of $21,000 million as a sign of generosity before Iraqi public opinion and the international community.

IRAQ AND THE THREAT OF A VICIOUS CIRCLE OF DEBT

Whether they are as high as 50, 100, or 200 billion dollars, the financial costs of Iraq are going to drag the country into a vicious circle of debt and therefore into a subordinate relationship with creditors, who will plunder oil reserves, with the United States helping themselves first.

To verify the value of this claim, let's try to calculate what reimbursing the debt would imply in the future. Imagine the following scenario: creditors agree to reduce their demands, and gauge the total amount of debt inherited from the pre-war period of March–April 2003 at around $62 billion (a one-third reduction), to which $50 billion in reparations would be added. Then several tens of billions in new debt linked to reconstruction would surely have to be added to that total, let's say $38 billion for 2003–5. Suppose that creditors postponed the beginning of repayment to 2005. In this hypothesis the total amount of debt and reparations weighing on Iraq would be around $150 billion.

How will the creditors set up the reimbursement plan? One plausible hypothesis is the following: they will demand that the completely broke Iraqi authorities use oil revenues for repayment, and here several other problems arise.

- First unknown factor: by 2005, will there be such Iraqi authorities with enough legitimacy to make commitments in the name of the State of Iraq (i.e. the Iraqi people)? This is far from certain.
- Second unknown factor: will oil production capacity have been fully re-established? In August 2003 production was barely at 300,000 barrels, compared with 1,700,000 before the 2003 war and 2,700,000 before the first Gulf War. The estimated cost of completely restoring oil production installations varies between $30–40 million. Who will pay? How will the security of those companies in charge of restoring and exploiting the fields be ensured?

According to the Financial Times (25 July 2003), the major oil companies have met with Bush administration representatives several times and have conveyed the message that it is out of the question for them to spend anything on restoring the production apparatus or on production itself as long as security cannot be guaranteed. Through Sir Philip Watts, president of Royal Dutch/Shell, transnational oil firms added that they themselves will determine when the future Iraqi regime meets the condition of legitimacy: 'When authorities that are legitimate in the eyes of the Iraqi people are in place, we will meet and recognize them!' In other words, the firms are telling the administration that the Iraqi authorities set up by the occupying troops do not meet the necessary conditions. Another part of the message is that they do indeed plan for the government to pay for the expense of restoring the production apparatus destroyed by the coalition. It is a real slap in the face for Bush.

- Third unknown factor: what will be the price of a barrel of oil in 2005?
- Fourth unknown factor: will the oil industry be publicly owned? If so, much of the revenue will go into the state's pockets, perhaps for debt reimbursement (should creditors so will it). This is a problem for the Bush administration's desire to privatize as many companies as possible. If the oil industry is privatized, the state will only make tax revenue from the proceeds, even though it is the body that will have to pay off $150 billion in debts.

According to various sources, in the very best (and very unlikely) scenario, oil revenues will hover around $10–20 billion in 2005. Now, how much will the reimbursement of $150 billion cost annually? Let's suppose that creditors will 'accept' a reimbursement plan at a preferential fixed interest rate of, say, 7 per cent over 20 years: $150 billion to be repaid over 20 years at 7 per cent represents an annual payment of about $18 billion (repayment on the interest and principal). In short, it's like trying to stuff a square peg in a round hole. It is utterly impossible based on export revenue of between $10–20 billion.

Where was the United States with this problem in mid-2003? A few days after the invasion of Iraq by American, British and Australian troops on 20 March 2003, George W. Bush estimated before Congress that the costs of the war for the US Treasury would be around $80 billion. On 7 September 2003 Bush declared to Congress that he was asking for $87 billion more. According to the PNUD and Unicef, $80 billion is exactly the extra sum needed each year over 10 years to guarantee universal access to drinkable water, basic education and healthcare (including nutrition), and gynaecological and obstetric care for all women for the entire planet. This sum – that no world summit of the last few years has managed to come up with (at Genoa in 2001 the G7 only raised a little under a billion dollars to fight AIDS, malaria, and tuberculosis) – the US government managed to raise and spend in a few months. The $80 billion Bush got from Congress, to which another $87 billion will now be added, was the same sum needed to destroy a certain amount of infrastructure and human life in Iraq and underwrite territorial occupation until the end of December 2003.

Now, confronting unexpected resistance, the US is having the worst kinds of difficulties. Sure, it is clearly dominant on the international scene. Sure, it's occupying the country. But it is hated by a large part of the population. US troops are constantly harassed. The cost of military occupation is much higher than foreseen; it is now at around $4 billion per month ($48 billion per year) for over 130,000 soldiers currently serving. The British are there with 11,000 troops, but the 30,000 that were supposed to be supplied by other alliance members have yet to show up.

This doesn't stop companies from the US and elsewhere from doing business. By the spring of 2003 the Halliburton Company (from Texas) was already on the ground doing emergency repairs to oil production equipment for a $7 billion contract. Dick Cheney, US vice-president, was the firm's CEO until August 2000.

Competitor Bechtel (responsible for water conflicts in Cochabamba in Bolivia) scored a $680 million contract for repairing the water and electricity distribution systems, as well as certain means of communication. Bechtel called a meeting in Washington in May 2003 on the theme 'How can a US company participate in reconstruction?' The 1,800 small and medium-sized businesses present cooled off considerably after being told that they would have to secure the safety of their employees and equipment themselves. Bechtel held the same kind of meeting in London and Kuwait City.

The big agro-chemical corporations, in particular the Anglo-Swiss transnational Syngenta, are also interested in the future of Iraq, as the country has traditionally been a big grain exporter. However, Monsanto has made it known that it isn't interested, perhaps because of other pressing issues elsewhere …

On site, administrator Paul Bremer is flashing all the neoliberal signals in order to draw investment; he has declared that everything must be privatized, that subsidies must be eliminated and private property rights increased. In exchange, he concedes the need for a social security safety net. We might get an idea of what he means by that when we remember that in May 2003, the United States paid 400,000 Iraqi workers and civil servants a monthly salary of $20, which adds up to $8 million total – 500 times less than what the US spends each month maintaining its own troops in Iraq.

CANCEL IRAQ'S ODIOUS DEBT AND PAY REPARATIONS

It's not because the US used the notion of odious debt in an opportunistic way that we should refuse to demand that it be applied in order to guarantee justice and fundamental rights for the Iraqi people. We must support the idea of a legitimate power in Iraq that could repudiate this debt. Reparation rights must also be broached. The cost must include the damage that the United States and other aggressors themselves never take into account: individual suffering, cultural pillage, etc., and for which they are nonetheless responsible since, as an occupying force, they are supposed to ensure the security of people and property.

Applying the odious debt doctrine to Iraq would be of utmost importance for the future of the Iraqi population, and beyond that, for a majority of the populations of indebted or so-called 'developing' nations. The citizens of these countries are perfectly within their rights to demand that a significant portion of their countries' debt be declared void based on the odious debt principle.

It belongs to the movement for another kind of globalization to demand that Iraq's external public debt be cancelled, combined with other demands, such as the withdrawal of occupation troops, the full exercise of their sovereignty by Iraqis themselves (which includes the use of their country's natural resources), and the payment of reparations to Iraqi citizens for the destruction and pillage suffered over the course of the war started by the American/British/Australian coalition in violation of the UN charter.

George W. Bush, Tony Blair, and Jon Howard, along with the heads of the Danish and Dutch governments (these countries participated directly in the invasion), should also be prosecuted as directly responsible for the crime of aggression, within the meaning given by the UN charter, and for war crimes.

As concerns proposals for Iraq's debt, we should push forward on the following points: the debt contracted under Saddam Hussein's regime is an odious debt and therefore void; a subsequent democratic regime should refuse to take responsibility for that debt and would have the right to repudiate it; new debts due to the costs of war and reconstruction are also odious and therefore void; the victims of Saddam Hussein, those of American aggression, of pillage, and the current occupation have the right to reparations. As for citizen action and the action of public authorities: we must participate in general mobilizations, in partitions like that of the Committee for the Abolition of Third World Debt. We must also demand audits from public authorities (not necessarily wait for them, but instead organize citizens' audits) on the debts that creditors are claiming against Iraq. What are they? Any creditor claiming reimbursement of a debt from Iraq must answer citizens' questions on the nature of these debts. In what contract are they defined? Who were the contracting parties? What were they for – arms? civilian equipment? What were the contract terms? What amounts have already been paid? Doing the research work here may help to show that the debts at stake are in fact odious.

9

The Creation of an Arbitration Tribunal on Debt: An Alternative Solution?

Hugo Ruiz Diaz[1] (CADTM)

This chapter presents a brief analysis of proposals for the creation of an international arbitration tribunal on debt, and is aimed at the international CADTM network, so as to better clarify our position and, at the same time, take the elements of such a tribunal to other activists. The chapter leaves aside analyses of the procedural aspects included in such proposals (who should launch the mechanism, who takes charge of the evidence, conditions in which debt may be considered illegitimate, conditions and mechanisms for civil society participation, etc.). The detailed debates on internal mechanisms and procedures are sufficiently developed in several proposals, notably those of Jubilee Germany, Jubilee UK and Acosta-Ugarteche.

This chapter therefore approaches the subject from the general characteristics of the proposals. It is important to note that these proposals are not, in principle, contradictory with the positions taken by CADTM. They are complementary in the process of struggle for the cancellation of third world debt.

THE PROPOSALS

Recently, CADTM has been confronted by three proposals. The first is that drawn up by Alejandro Bendana (Nicaragua) for Jubilee South (disseminated to the World Social Forum in Porto Alegre in January 2003 and the March 2003 AITEC meeting in Paris). At the time of writing, it is not known whether this represents an official Jubilee South document. This text is entitled 'Repudiation and arbitration: The need for an integral approach?' and is available in French.

There is also a proposal presented by Alberto Acosta and Oscar Ugarteche at a seminar on Latin American debt in Brussels in May 2003 and also a Jubilee Iraq (UK) proposal presented by Justin Alexander in Geneva with respect to the Iraqi debt.

All the proposals which have been put forward aim at a real solution to the foreign debt problem of the third world. They all have the same foundation: legal accountability (that is, the possibility of bringing a case) before an international body. Substantively, they entail the creation of independent international arbitration proceedings which recognize the respective responsibilities of debtors and creditors. As a general rule, the renegotiation of foreign debt has taken place under the authority of creditors.

In view of the seriousness of the debt problem, the creation of an arbitration tribunal would seem a more realistic proposal than the outright cancellation of debt pure and simple (clearly just, but ineffective, in the view of the authors cited above). Thus the proposals seek a fundamental solution, using means which are entirely normal and traditional in international law: arbitration, an institution widely used by states and the private sector, notably in matters of international private commercial law. In this respect, it is noteworthy that arbitration constitutes a much more flexible form of jurisdiction, with less burdensome procedures and thus greater accessibility, relative to other types of tribunal. Moreover, the cost of such proceedings would be borne by state governments, including those of the poorest countries.

The proposals are even more attractive if one takes into account the fact that loan contracts signed between private creditors and states, between states and international financial institutions (IFIs), or between states, generally anticipate recourse to tribunals or judicial organs outside the jurisdiction of the debtor country. The proposals envisage the use of a jurisdiction characterized in principle by neutrality, and intended to be more beneficial to the debtor country. Ultimately, the intention is to correct an unequal and inequitable legal relationship.

REASONS FOR AN ARBITRATION TRIBUNAL ON DEBT

One of the characteristics of the proposals is that they call for an independent tribunal in which civil society would play an important role. Given the nature of dispute settlement clauses between debtors and creditors and the law applicable to them, debtors are always at a disadvantage. It should be noted that, in the case of the International Monetary Fund (IMF) and the World Bank, disputes with respect to debt are settled by the institutions themselves.

A second characteristic refers to the problem of finding a balance between debtors and creditors. In fact, it is normal to find dispute settlement clauses under which states explicitly renounce national courts in favour of foreign courts. This transfer of competence is normally in favour of courts in the US (as in the case of the dispute settlement clause between Argentina, private creditors and the IFI) or in the UK. It is precisely to avoid situations where creditors act both as judges and parties in a dispute that these proposals are presented as credible alternatives. IFIs themselves are creditors who have a strong interest in perpetuating unequal creditor–debtor relations.

As already indicated, the proposals entail using a judicial mechanism widely accepted by states, IFIs and private creditors. Civil society actors, like states, will be enabled to present their demands to the tribunal.

THE COMPETENCE OF THE INTERNATIONAL ARBITRATION TRIBUNAL AND POSSIBLE CONSEQUENCES

The central point which the international arbitration tribunal on debt (IATD) should consider is the evaluation of a country's overall debt, in order to establish which part is legitimate and which part is illegitimate. Among other things, the IATD should pronounce on debts:

- contracted by illegitimate debtors or illegal regimes, or by creditors which acted illegitimately or illegally in collusion with the governments of debtor countries;
- contracted for illegitimate or illegal purposes (war, oppression of the population, etc.);

- contracted by democratic governments but closely linked with corruption; which violate human rights (economic, social, cultural, civil, political).

Thus, beyond the legal aspect, the IATD could consider not only the illegality of debts, but also their legitimacy.

PRACTICAL DIFFICULTIES

What appears simple in principle may nonetheless be extremely difficult to put into practice.

Any tribunal, as a judicial organ of international law, must be given its own competence. In the case of the IATD, it would have to rule on the validity or illegality (and potentially on the illegitimacy) of the debt contracted by a state, which could lead to the nullification of a particular debt. Would the creditors (public and private) submit themselves to a jurisdiction which could lead to the nullification of debts contracted by certain governments? Equally, the debt problem is closely linked with the corruption of southern governments, which places them in a difficult situation, since the analysis would be concerned with the legality or legitimacy of their debts. Would they accept that a decision would equally signify government corruption in the process of borrowing and the implementation of privatization? The tribunal thus exceeds the purely judicial to become, strictly, political in nature.

The creation of any international tribunal raises, in international law, the issue of the willingness of the debtors and creditors. They are the subjects of law who can take such an initiative and bring it to a conclusion in a treaty or agreement. Thus the creation of any international tribunal must necessarily pass through the stages of negotiation, conclusion and ratification of a treaty. In practice all this implies, and international law provides for, bitter negotiations between the parties concerned. In the particular case of the IATD, its creation requires prior negotiations between states, and between them and IFIs, also subject to international law. This is where the juridical figure of debtor/creditor is brought to bear. A fundamental question remains to be resolved: what status to accord the private creditors. The Acosta-Ugarteche proposal entails referring the creation of the IATD to the UN General Assembly, where the negotiations would be conducted. At present, there are more than 160 UN member states. However, wherever the proposal is made, the initiative would always be that of states or an IFI. In the latter case, it seems unlikely that it would take or support such an initiative.

Equally, the basis of international law concerning treaties is essentially voluntary (until now, at least). It is governed by the 1969 Vienna Convention on the Law of Treaties between States and the 1985 Vienna Convention.

This voluntary nature means that states can participate or refuse to participate in negotiations prior to the conclusion of the IATD. Moreover, if such a convention or agreement were concluded, states and IFIs could equally refuse to sign or ratify it. Under the 1969 Vienna Convention, states and international organizations which do not sign, do not ratify or do not become parties to it remain third parties. As a result, they are not legally bound by it. Consider this: if an IFI, the US or the EU member states refused to ratify or be parties to such an accord, they would remain third parties, and the IATD could not exercise its competence in relation to them. There is a very high risk that an IFI or certain of the more powerful Western countries may not participate in the IATD negotiation process, may not ratify it or be parties to it.

There is a co-responsibility between southern governments, IFIs and private creditors in the process of indebtedness. In principle, these governments, though already having at their disposal the legal means not to pay their foreign debts, have not used them. These same governments would have to put in place an international arbitration tribunal on debt in collaboration with IFIs.

With regard to IFIs, the proposals do not contain references (at least not explicitly developed as yet) concerning the international responsibility of IFIs and/or private creditors. For CADTM, this issue is an essential element for calling into question, on the one hand, the legitimacy of IFI policies, and on the other hand the constant and permanent violation of international law resulting from the application of those policies. Raising the issue of the international responsibility of IFIs and private banks is a matter of primary importance, where civil society and citizens' groups have the initiative, and not governments.

There is another fundamental problem, which has not yet been subject to detailed analysis. What, in fact, would be the law applicable to the IATD? International law? The domestic law of debtor countries, or that of creditor countries? Both? And – for private creditors – international commercial law or the domestic law of debtor countries? The definition of the applicable law is not simply a technical legal issue, but essentially a political problem.

A very important issue for CADTM is that of individual criminal responsibility and the responsibility of moral persons for serious violations of international law; for example, the collusion of IFIs and private creditors with the Argentinean dictatorship (responsible for the worst kind of crimes against humanity), or that of transnational companies with the apartheid regime in South Africa. This is a question which exceeds the competence of the IATD, unless the states and the IFIs party to such an agreement decide otherwise or consider that the norms which will govern their competence come under jus cogens or imperative norms, which takes us back to international criminal law.

CADTM'S POSITION

CADTM has taken a firm view on the illegitimacy, illegality and nullity of third world debts. According to the accepted position, it is a question of policies imposed on peoples by the dominant states and the IFIs. In our view, it is about illegitimate institutions implementing policies in favour of transnational capital, so as to submit peoples to their domination. Thus, CADTM appropriates international law to call into question the policies of the IFIs, their legitimacy and the legality of their actions. In this way, CADTM directly proposes that their activities should be deemed criminal, including those of private creditors and Western governments.

In this respect, CADTM deserves praise for exploiting the OLMOS Sentence of July 2000, which shows the criminal machinations and the criminal organizational behaviour of the IFIs, and the illicit conduct of private creditors. The development and adaptation of the doctrine of odious debt points in the same direction.

For CADTM, the debt problem, and the application of policies linked to it, is not a one-way street. Rather, there is also responsibility, complicity and corruption within the dominant elites of most third world states. These are the same dominant elites who benefit directly from the policies of indebtedness and who are responsible for applying the policies dictated by IFIs. Thus, there is every reason to use the appropriate legal instruments available to citizens to start proceedings aimed at recovering the funds diverted by corrupt leaders. There are numerous precedents.

THE INTERNATIONAL RESPONSIBILITY OF IFIS AND PRIVATE CREDITORS AND THE OBLIGATION OF REPARATION

Put simply, international responsibility, including criminal responsibility, is of primary importance. Research on and debates about international law show that the policies imposed by the IFIs, like the machinations of the governments at the centre and periphery of the world system, are substantially contrary to the obligations imposed by international law, particularly those relating to the protection of human rights in a broad sense.

Emphasizing international responsibility implies that the policies of indebtedness of the third world constitute permanent and constant violations of international law – that is, illicit acts. Moreover, whatever the system in place in a particular state, our research has shown that international law (including the Statutes of the World Bank, for example) places obligations on IFIs to exercise due vigilance and diligence to ensure that their activities do not lead to violations of international law (notably relating to civil, political, economic and social rights), including the need to ensure that loans extended to governments are not used to buy arms to commit genocide, for example.

The obligation of reparation is a logical consequence of IFI policies which violate international law. It is not a question of negotiating the conditions in which debt is licit or illicit; since the policies are substantially contrary to international law (permanent violation of economic and social rights, for example), IFIs and private creditors are under an obligation to provide compensation for the consequences of such violations.

INTERNATIONAL CRIMINAL LAW

In the criminal domain, recourse to the rules of international criminal law, in particular to those applied by the Nuremberg Trials, but also to those which are widely incorporated in state legal systems, allows us to point to IFIs as criminal organizations, since they have acted in full knowledge and in collaboration with criminal regimes, thus becoming accomplices in serious violations of international law: forced disappearances, large-scale torture, extra-judicial killings, rape, etc.

THE CHOSEN PATH: RECOURSE TO DOMESTIC AND INTERNATIONAL LAW

Unlike proposals on the IATD (an international legal organ which would have to be the result of negotiations between debtors and creditors), CADTM has deliberately chosen recourse to the domestic law of states, whose foundation is constituted by international law. Ultimately, it is a question of how to begin legal proceedings when a state's law allows such recourse.

This choice responds to the need to give citizens who are victims of the policies of the banks and IFIs the basic formal legal instruments to initiate enforceable proceedings. It is important to note that this choice is based on recent precedents, such as complaints against multinationals for serious violations of international law (the Ogonis of Nigeria against Shell; the complaint against Total Fina in Belgium for complicity in crimes against humanity in Burma; the complaint by South African citizens against 21 multinationals for complicity in the crimes of the apartheid regime, among others). The importance of these complaints is that they throw light on the criminal activities of multinationals. Would this be so in an international court like the IATD?

These complaints, while they concern multinationals (which are totally different from IFIs under international law), can only reinforce the choice of targeting IFIs.

CADTM also raises the issue of the criminal responsibility of top executives of IFIs and creditor banks. These executives should be identified publicly (the law allows this) as accomplices who deliberate provide the financial means for criminal regimes that have committed crimes against humanity.

CADTM believes citizens' groups will take the lead. They should not have to depend on the good will of their states for the violation of their rights to be recognized as an injustice. Moreover, there is no guarantee that any final agreement will not be emptied of its original meaning without their full participation.

The creation of the IATD in not incompatible with the search for other means of cancelling foreign debt. It is citizens' movements which propose it, as one among many tools in the struggle against the policies imposed by IFIs. Our own specific recourse to the domestic legal system allows us to avoid the problem of dependence on international negotiations between states, and between international organizations, towards the conclusion of a treaty on the creation of the IATD.

1 Working translation from French by David Woodward.

10

Foreign Debt … Ecological Debt … Odious Debt

Aurora Donoso (Accion Ecologica)

Odious debt is debt contracted against the interests of the people of a given country, without consent, in the full knowledge of the creditor. This chapter will show how foreign debt that has spawned social and ecological debt is illicit. The terms of such debt, its conditions and purpose, and its serious impact, make it odious.

TIED LOANS

Foreign debt in Ecuador was born of the oil industry. Indeed, the oil boom in the 1970s heralded a new stage in foreign debt. According to the economist Alberto Acosta, between 1971 and 1981, foreign debt in Ecuador grew nearly 22-fold, rising from $260.8 million to $5,869.8 million.

Oil became collateral for loans. However, in the 1980s, the debt crisis occurred and interest rates were unilaterally increased by creditors: foreign debt became the main tool whereby international financial institutions (IFIs) maintained the flow of natural and financial resources from the South to the North, imposing on countries in the South the neoliberal policies that suited the interests of the North and tailoring loans according to their financial and commercial interests.

As of the 1980s, IFIs fostered a new oil boom in Ecuador through Letters of Intent with the International Monetary Fund and World Bank Country Assistance Strategies (CAS), the prerequisites for gaining access to new loans. The IMF promoted greater oil production to produce surpluses with which to pay interest on foreign debt. Projects like the HCP in Ecuador – the heavy crude pipeline designed to double oil production in indigenous territories and protected areas in the Ecuadorian Amazon – are set out in the Letter of Intent with the IMF: 70 per cent of the resources obtained through the HCP will be earmarked for foreign debt reduction.

WHAT IS ECOLOGICAL DEBT?

Ecological debt is the social and environmental impact (mainly in countries in the South) caused by the intensive tapping of natural resources like oil, gas, coal and minerals, to sustain production and consumption in the industrialized countries of the North. It is the social and environmental damage caused by implementation of the 'Green Package' for single export crops that threaten the food production and cultural sovereignty of communities and peoples in the South. It is the intellectual appropriation and use of ancestral knowledge about seeds, medicinal plants and other resources, which underpin biotechnology and modern agro-industry. It is the air pollution created by the industrialized countries owing to their disproportionate emissions of gases, the main cause of global warming and the depletion of the ozone layer. It is the responsibility borne by industrialized countries in the production of chemical, biological and nuclear weapons and toxic substances and waste that are stored in countries in the South.

FOREIGN DEBT AND ECOLOGICAL DEBT

The oil industry is a good example of the relation between foreign and ecological debt.

It is worth mentioning that the IMF and its institutions put pressure on countries in the South to increase the exploitation of their natural resources in order to pay foreign debt. To this end, the International Bank grants our countries loans to build infrastructure to enhance the use of these resources.

The serious social and environmental impact of the oil and mining industry in the world is recognized worldwide. The impact is both local and global. We have examples of oil-related ecological debt in Asia, Africa and Latin America. Countries like Burma, Thailand, Chad, Sudan, Nigeria, Colombia and Ecuador have been seriously affected by transnational oil companies like Shell, Chevron/Texaco, Exxon Mobil, Total/Fina/Elf, AGIP, British Petroleum, Unocal, Occidental, and many others. These companies have destroyed and polluted nature and adversely affected cultures, particularly those of the indigenous, black, rural and fishing communities – peoples like the Kofan, Secoya and Huaorani in Ecuador, the Mapuche in Chile, Guahibos and Araucas in Colombia, Uchaur, Urarina, and Yora in Peru, Sakai and Aceh in Indonesia, Karen in Burma, Ogoni in Nigeria, Bakola in Cameroon, rural peoples in Chad, ethnic minorities in Sudan, all the people in the Niger Delta, and many others.

It is enough to look at the ecological debt of Texaco in Ecuador to understand the very serious impact of the oil industry on the country, which has gone so far as to accelerate the disappearance of indigenous peoples in the Amazon, their knowledge and their culture.

Other examples that illustrate the close link between foreign debt and ecological debt include loans designed to change national legislation and foster mining activities. For example, in 1996, the World Bank earmarked US$643 million for mining projects. In Ecuador alone, the World Bank, with co-financing from the governments of Sweden and the UK, lent US$24 million to develop industrial mining, including a new Mining Law to promote foreign investment in Ecuador.

Other loans were designed to change agricultural policies and traditional farming systems through massive use of the Green Package and agro-industrial technology, in addition to promoting food exports. In Ecuador alone, between 1985 and 1988, more than US$600 million worth of loans were obtained from the World Bank and IDB to this end – loans that benefited the international companies which produce pesticides, seed and machinery, provide advisory services and market produce abroad.

These loans benefited international creditors and national elites, generating foreign currency to service the debt, but, above all, deepening social and ecological debts. This is the case of the shrimp, flower and African palm industries, together with non-traditional export products that seriously affect the health of workers and pollute the soil, air and water.

ODIOUS DEBT

Three conditions must be met for a debt to be considered odious:

1 The nation has not given its general consent to the debt.

2 The funds borrowed are to be used in a manner that runs counter to the interests of the nation.
3 The creditor made the loan in full knowledge of the above.

As of the1980s, the loans taken out by Ecuador met the conditions laid down by the IMF and the interests of the IFIs, companies and governments which have helped to increase poverty and damage the environment on a local and global level. The mere fact these kinds of terms are met makes the debts illicit. What is more, if we take into account the now obvious social, environmental and cultural damage, we should not only view such debts as unlawful and odious, but also demand reparation. It is obvious that the nation did not give its general consent to these loans; it merely responded to the pressure and conditions of IFIs; and these latter (that is, the creditors) were fully aware of it.

As for the borrowed funds, rather than being used in the country's interests, the loans are designed to benefit creditors and their vested interests, at a cost of deepened poverty for our peoples and the pillaging of our land. It is enough to look at migration and poverty indicators to realize that the loans ran counter to the interests of the nation, even if phrases like 'development', 'sustainable development', 'poverty alleviation', 'development assistance' and 'protecting the poor' are always included in agreements.

According to Eric Toussaint, each year the countries of the third world pay US$240,000 million to service foreign debt. Ecuador alone allocates $2,200 million a year to pay interest on foreign debt.

According to the ILO, over 120 million immigrants moved from Latin America, Africa and Asia to countries in the North in the 1990s. And this trend is increasing. Just between May and July 2003, over 300,000 Ecuadorian men and women migrated to the USA and Europe, mainly Spain and Italy.

In 1995, 56 per cent of the population in Ecuador lived in poverty, an excessively high figure that has now risen to 79 per cent. The rural population is most deeply affected.

Other indicators that these loans have benefited neither the country nor its people are to be found in the serious environmental impact of activities that seek intensively to tap natural resources like oil, minerals, wood, gas and coal: deforestation, loss of biodiversity, river and soil pollution, destruction of peoples and cultures. Health has been damaged as a result of single-export crops and the use of the Green Package and its technology.

Loans have promoted a concentration in land ownership, spawning displacement, exploitation and poverty, mainly among indigenous peoples and rural and black communities.

Loans generate poverty, and the results are there to see. They seek primarily to maintain the flow of financial resources, natural resources and cheap labour from the South to the North to sustain patterns of production, consumption and waste production that endanger the survival of local populations, their cultures, diversity and the planet in general.

There is no doubt that foreign debt which creates ecological debt is odious debt!

11

Not Just Being Right, But Getting Justice, Or: How to Get the Ball in the Back of the Net

Jürgen Kaiser (ErlassJahr 2000)

International debtor–creditor relations are a lot like street football: there is a lot of shouting, the rules are never quite clear, and at the end of the day it's goals that count. In previous chapters we saw that there are many good reasons to question the legitimacy of the claims of the creditors of the North against the debtors of the South, and we have also seen that critical and well-founded doubts regarding the legitimacy of claims have not, so far, led to their genuine cancellation.

How, then, to get illegitimate claims waived, or how to get the ball in the back of the net?

It is not a goal simply when the public cheers – even if 60,000 people see the ball between the goal posts. When powerful social movements clamour for illegitimate claims to be waived, virtually without exception governments and central banks keep counting, to see if there is any way for them to recoup the money. It is not even a goal when the ball is objectively behind the line – when it has been proved to creditors that the elites of a debtor country have broken the law and been judged by national courts, such as in the case of the Argentine junta. Here too, they keep counting.

It is only a goal when the referee says it is!

The problem with international debt management, as with a game of street football, is that there is no referee. Or rather, there is but, as some of you might remember, in the street the rules are decided either by the owner of the ball, who otherwise can take the ball and leave the game, spoiling everybody's fun, or by the biggest and strongest player, who if necessary can back up their interpretation of the rules with some forceful arguments.

Relations between international debtors and creditors work in much the same way. When there is a need for negotiations, because the debtor either cannot or does not want to pay, the debtor must bring the case before a committee like the Paris Club, created and controlled by the creditors and owners of the ball (i.e. of the loaned capital), who if necessary have the means, ranging from gunboats to economic sanctions, to implement their rules and determine if and how much the debtor has to pay.

In fora of this kind creditors overcome their problems – albeit inadequately – themselves: when it becomes clear that you really can't get any more out of the pockets of a naked person (i.e. an extremely poor debtor country), they then arrange limited concessions. In the Paris Club the question of the legitimacy of claims is only asked on a formal level. Only if the signature on the dotted line underneath the credit agreement cannot be attributed to any authorized signatory for the debtor country can pressure from rival creditors lead to some of the claims against the debtor country not being recognized. The Club calls this process 'verification of claims'; it comes right at the very beginning of the debt relief procedure.

URGENT: REFEREE NEEDED

If it is going to be possible to question the legitimacy of claims in future, the first thing we need is a referee worthy of the name; somebody who is not themselves a party and who will not be made richer or poorer by the decision. That means no more and no less than fundamentally questioning the division of power between debtors and creditors, or more specifically, the monopoly on power and decisions that creditors have enjoyed up until now.

To this end, www.erlassjahr.de is calling for the existing procedure to be replaced with a 'fair and transparent arbitration procedure' (FTAP), which would mean that decisions as to how much and when debtors have to pay would be made by neither the debtor nor the creditor, but by a neutral authority. In practice, this could be a small arbitration court, comprising an equal number of adjudicators from both sides, who would then appoint one other judge. This arbitration court would – as in a normal court in a functioning state based on the rule of law – have full control over the procedure, and its decisions would be based on laws and rights, which means rules that have been verifiably and bindingly established before the beginning of the hearing with regard to the question of the legitimacy of claims.

HOW WOULD IT WORK IN PRACTICE?

The FTAP comprises multiple stages, from a debtor government's application for a hearing, to the establishment of the arbitration court, the testimony of all those concerned, and the arbitration court's ruling on the debtor's proposal. The legitimacy of claims can be questioned at three stages of this process:

1. In the FTAP, as in the Paris Club, 'verification of claims' should occur at the beginning of the procedure. In any event this does not fall to the Paris Club secretariat, which is nothing more than a department of the French ministry of finance, but is incumbent on a small staff of technical experts, established in a neutral institution and thus removed from the influence of either of the two parties. At this early stage, that technical staff can raise doubts about the creditors' claims in the formal analysis. The technical experts naturally cannot take decisions, only make recommendations on which the arbitration court appointed by the two parties will then rule.
2. Following the verification of claims and the establishment of the arbitration court, the parties (i.e. the debtor government and the creditor) testify. Both the debtor and any creditor who wishes to call into question the claims of other creditors has the opportunity to raise doubts as to the legitimacy of individual claims. However, the arbitration court only reaches its decision after a third stage has been completed.
3. Once the debtor and creditors have testified, third parties also have an opportunity to give their views on the question of payment or non-payment. In the Paris Club this privilege has until now been restricted to a

few international organizations, such as the World Bank or UNCTAD, who often intercede for a solution that favours the debtor country, but never on the basis of doubts over the legitimacy of the claims. In the FTAP this right to be heard, which is comparable with Chapter 9 of the US Legal Code (bankruptcy of municipalities), is extended to a larger circle of 'concerned parties'. In this way social movements, churches and unions can not only give their opinions, which would mean the cancellation of claims for the people of the debtor country (or the employees of a creditor bank, for example), but can also critically challenge the legitimacy of creditors' claims. The extent to which the court of arbitration would then heed them would depend on the quality of the evidence submitted to them proving crooked business, corruption, deliberate planning or political scheming. In all cases the final decision remains the privilege of the arbitration court.

IT'S NOT JUST ABOUT CLEARING UP AFTERWARDS

A procedure of this kind, which cannot be controlled by either of the two parties, will not just serve to ensure that old illegitimate claims find their way into the dustbin where they belong. The prospect of having to publicly answer a few unwelcome questions about the quality of the projects they finance, the bank charges levied or their knowledge of the borrower's economic situation, is the only effective means of deterring creditors from employing that kind of lending in the future.

12

A Fair and Transparent Arbitration Mechanism

Comité Catholique contre la Faim et pour le Développement

Increasingly severe financial crises have now become one of the major threats to development. So far, the international financial institutions (IFIs), in particular the International Monetary Fund (IMF) whose job it is, have been unable to respond effectively: being subject to the interests of the rich countries who are their main shareholders and locked into a neoliberal free market ideology, they have difficulty putting in place the regulations that are needed. Yet their very survival is at stake. The causes of financial crises like that in Argentina are manifold: financial speculation, lack of transparency, the volatility of financing, and capital flight. However, it is debt, or to be more precise over-indebtedness, that lies at the heart of the structural financial problems which these countries are experiencing. In the case of Argentina, foreign debt stands at $142 billion, and the social and economic cost is structurally endangering the financial and currency stability of the country. Suspending repayments is one of the first measures taken to stop the haemorrhaging. But what should be the next step? A country's situation once it has recovered (particularly at the political level) its ability to negotiate with the creditors to reduce the burden of repayments, which in any case cannot be completely certain? How can over-indebtedness crises be averted?

PROBLEMS WITH CURRENT INTERNATIONAL DEBT MANAGEMENT

The mechanisms for managing international debt that creditors have put into place successively since the 1980s have broadly proven their inability to resolve the debt crisis in the countries of the South. Particularly within the Paris Club, all of these mechanisms, like the current enhanced Heavily Indebted Poor Countries initiative (HIPC II), were presented in their time as a means of resolving the problem once and for all, but in the end turned out to be incapable of lifting the countries concerned out of the spiral of debt. The underlying reason for these successive failures is not so much the result of any particular relief plan as the way in which these plans were defined.

The problem is above all structural and stems from the imbalance in the relations between creditors and debtors when they are negotiating international debt. In fact, the competent authorities in this process are both judges and parties to it, incapable of working for the common good and even less so of defending the most vulnerable. They are either groups of creditors (the Paris Club, the London Club), or credit authorities controlled by creditor countries (IFIs). It is the creditors who select the process, set the rules and, on the basis of analysis that they have commissioned or produced themselves, finally decide what should be done, taking into account their own interests.

Creditor countries or institutions have always seemed rather more concerned with monitoring the financial system (the risk of the chain bankruptcy of private banks, non-repayment of multilateral credit, etc.) than with alleviating the burden on the poorest countries. Creditors, and more specifically the IFIs, have even fed the spiral of over-indebtedness in the South with 'defensive loans' intended to cover the repayments on earlier loans, in order to protect the interests of the financial actors.

Negotiations are controlled by public creditors

The experience of the Paris Club is particularly telling: there, the creditors assume the role of judge, deliberating in secret on the basis of evaluations made by the IFIs which they control, before summoning the debtor countries and presenting them with a fait accompli.

As a result of this stranglehold over the decision-making process, the public creditors can be content to take measures against debtor countries that are designed to best protect their own interests. This generally means repeated rescheduling, in order to recover as much of their loans as possible, regardless of the consequences for debtor countries. Moreover, the creditors' situation allows them to impose on debtor countries the economic policies that they wish them to pursue – particularly policies for structural change. The relationship is therefore essentially based on the power, or even control, of the rich countries over developing countries.

Yet the lender and the borrower have a shared responsibility for the accumulation of debt. All too often, loans have been granted with a view to defending the political and economic interests of the moneylenders or of a corrupt minority in the South acting in the interests of those same moneylenders, rather than in the interests of the population. Similarly, the rich countries bear considerable responsibility for the accumulation of debt that has arisen from the lack of adequate aid or the continued deterioration of the terms of exchange.

Private creditors pool their losses

Similarly, the lack of a regulatory mechanism encourages private creditors (commercial banks, private investment funds, etc.) to behave irresponsibly both in legal and economic terms, in contrast to national legal systems, which supervise creditors' actions and bestow obligations on them towards their debtors. These creditors are assured of recouping their stake and even of reaping substantial rewards, regardless of their share of the risk, leaving the populations of debtor countries to pay the exorbitant social cost.

The current framework, going against even the liberal principles of the market economy to which these actors refer, allows private creditors not to assume the risks that they have taken. Whenever creditors' ill-considered investments, favoured in particular by the liberalization of capital flows, contribute to the emergence of an over-indebtedness crisis, the IMF's bailout programmes every time assure them a return on their investment, at the expense of a renewed inflation of that country's public debt. Indeed, these bailout programmes implemented by the IMF are always in line with the interests of the main creditor countries.

This economic aberration, described by economists as 'moral hazard', is a real ethical scandal. It violates the conventional principles of contract law, which imply that contracting parties have a shared responsibility. Moreover, this moral hazard contravenes existing national-level banking law, which obligates bankers to exercise caution when granting loans. So, when a business goes bankrupt, lenders are forced to assume their share of the risk. If a debtor ceases repayment, they then have to draw a line under a part of their debt. This means that when a company like Enron is declared bankrupt, it can invoke the protection of Article 11 of the American bankruptcy code, despite embezzlement by its directors.

In contrast, private creditors can lend irresponsibly to the countries of the South without the risk of financial penalty, even if a financial crisis erupts and plunges the country into social chaos. Similarly, under pressure from the financial markets, the public authorities in debtor countries have often been forced to assume debt incurred by private actors so that private creditors are able to recoup their funds, despite the non-viability of their investments, so as to avoid or at least delay a financial crisis.

The problems arising from the lack of an appropriate regulatory mechanism have acquired an extra dimension in the last decade or so, with the financial markets' greater involvement in the external financing of middle-income countries (essentially countries labelled 'emerging'), through bonds. This phenomenon encourages purely speculative loan management.

Private creditors are now numerous, anonymous, and sometimes even prefer unstable situations in order to be able to speculate better on discounted loans. This is contributing to the emergence of a worrying phenomenon in speculative funds known as 'vulture funds'. These vulture creditors buy bad debts at knock-down prices and then recover the entirety of their initial value, as well as subsequent interest, through the courts. They make huge profits like this, to the detriment of the restructuring agreements that are negotiated by debtor countries having difficulty. These vulture funds will prey on any developing country, including some extremely poor countries.

The persistence of the debt crisis in developing countries highlights the impasse that is the result of the lack of a formal mechanism for restructuring sovereign debt. A sustainable response to this problem will entail establishing a fair and transparent judicial mechanism that takes into account the economic future of the indebted country and respects the basic needs of their populations.

THE INTERNATIONAL INSOLVENCY MECHANISM PROPOSED BY THE IMF

Establishing a formal mechanism for restructuring sovereign debt

The deadlock in which Argentina has found itself underlines more than ever the economic and social damage that is being caused for want of an insolvency procedure at the international level. This crisis is one of several in a number of developing countries whose debt has reached an intolerable level.

In fact, by opposing this kind of procedure until very recently, the creditor countries have been inflicting considerable damage on their debtors. As Professor Kunibert Raffer, for example, says, 'the difference between bankruptcy procedures and the management (as currently practiced) of over-indebtedness crises is very simple. There is a contradiction between the arbitrary power of the creditors who use their dominant position to keep their debtors under control on the one hand, and the modern laws protecting all human beings to which the creditor countries of the North claim to subscribe on the other.'

A formal mechanism for restructuring sovereign debt, which can be applied to states when they are incapable of repaying their debt, has been proven necessary for an economically effective and socially acceptable management of over-indebtedness crises. If Argentina had had recourse to such a mechanism, the financial crisis to which it fell victim could have been prevented, as the IMF has somewhat belatedly admitted. In particular, having this legal instrument would make it possible to force the many private creditors to agree to concessions by a majority. The resulting agreement would then apply to all creditors, including those who had refused to negotiate (known as 'rogue' creditors).

For this sort of mechanism to be viable it must be accompanied by the suspension of all repayments and control over capital flows. These defensive methods would guarantee protection for debtor countries in difficulty against speculative assaults and capital flight. Moreover, private creditors would be forced to negotiate a restructuring of their loans, whereas until now they have been very little involved in the management of over-indebtedness crises.

Clearly, for the mechanism to be effective, creditors will no longer be able to have recourse to their national judicial systems in order to pursue debtor countries who have ceased repayments. In addition to adding new clauses to loan agreements, the legislative route to achieving this would be signing an international treaty or a commitment from all states to amend their national legislation. These major changes would require immense political will, but are vital for the establishment of international regulations.

The IMF's proposal

The IMF now says it supports the establishment of a restructuring mechanism accompanied by a moratorium on repayments and controls over exchanges in order to prevent capital flight. For the IMF, adopting this position constitutes a radical change and is an implicit acknowledgement of the failure of the deregulated model of capital flows that it has favoured for more than twenty years. However, the IMF's proposal is far from satisfactory. In reality, the IMF's motives are once again not so much the common good as protecting the interests of its main shareholders. In fact, the rich countries, and primarily the United States, are above all seeking a way to avoid having to pay out considerable sums in the event of a financial crisis.

The IMF's proposal is for the moment only at the consideration stage and there is no reason to think that it will succeed. Nonetheless, in response to criticism from civil society organizations (CSOs), the IMF has moved away from its initial position and there do seem to be some positive aspects:

- The preventative nature of this mechanism with regard to private creditors, who would find themselves involved in the management of financial crises, making them responsible and thus undermining the moral hazards argument.
- Unlike in the bankruptcy procedures that apply to businesses, it is the

debtor countries that initiate this 'temporary bankruptcy' by declaring a moratorium on their repayments. This means that their unique situation as a sovereign debtor is taken into account (after the model of Article 9 of the American bankruptcy code, which applies to sovereign debtors and local municipalities). It therefore also gives states leverage with private creditors. The states concerned would therefore be able to impose temporary controls over capital flows.
- Although it was designed primarily for emerging economies, the IMF seems to have developed a wider interpretation in the wake of the Argentine crisis by addressing the possibility of extending the mechanism to apply to the poorest countries.

The IMF is planning to establish 'an international entity able to arbitrate in disagreements and supervise negotiations'. However, we have to be careful that the authority thought up by the IMF is truly independent.

Despite the significant progress that has been made regarding the current legal vacuum, the IMF, as you might expect, has reserved a key place for itself in the process. This does not fundamentally address the imbalance in the current system. There are even legitimate grounds to ask whether the IMF's main objective in making this proposal isn't to limit its own financial implication in financial crises.

Although the process is set in motion at the initiative of states, the IMF's approval is required. The IMF argues that this sort of control is needed in order to prevent the mechanism being hijacked by unwarranted demands. However, since this control takes priority, the effect of one of the interested parties having this blocking power would be a distortion of the insolvency procedure itself. Moreover, it is very likely that in this context the geopolitical and economic interests of the rich countries (particularly the United States) would take priority over all other considerations. Therefore, if a procedure of this kind is set up, the task of considering and approving a country's request, if this is required, should be carried out by a technical secretariat under the auspices of the United Nations.

The IMF is insistent on its status as a 'priority creditor', by virtue of it being the 'last resort lender'. But there is no logical relationship between this status and the protection of new loans intended to give debtors renewed liquidity within the restructuring or relief period.

The IMF always restricts itself to a strictly financial analysis on the basis of solvency criteria. It does not consider the alternative proposals put forward by CSOs, which try to take into account the international objectives for human development and the fight against poverty when evaluating debt relief needs.

The proposal also has serious shortcomings in terms of transparency and the involvement of civil society, which are vital to establishing a genuinely democratic process.

Further to these various points, the crux of the debate is in the nature of the decision-making process. The mechanism that has been proposed is one that tends towards facilitating and supervising negotiations between the various interested parties. The power of decision therefore remains in their hands. The fundamental imbalance is not challenged. On the contrary, one of the perverse effects of the mechanism could in fact be to put over-indebted countries even further under the IMF's tutelage.

The role of the independent authority would be restricted to facilitating the hearing, supervising the agreement reached between debtors and creditors, and resolving or arbitrating differences of opinion as to the interpretation or implementation of the agreement. The authority is therefore not a judicial authority (permanent or ad hoc) with power of decision. There are two reasons for the IMF's reluctance: firstly, in limiting the authority's role, the Fund is responding to pressure from private creditors, who categorically reject the idea of an external market regulator able to impose a solution, if necessary without their consent. Secondly, we also have to recognize that all existing insolvency mechanisms (including Article 9 of the American bankruptcy code) work on this principle. The judges essentially play the role of facilitators.

THE STATE OF THE DEBATE WITHIN THE G7

The American position

Motivated by a desire to reduce the financial implications for the IMF when countries with emerging economies suffer financial crises, the US government initially said it supported the IMF's proposal. But no sooner had a section of the administration refused to enhance the IMF's role (the current government is seeking to disengage) than pressure from financial groups caused the United States to do an about-turn. To oppose this project, the United States now proposes a 'market-regulated approach', ruling out the option of setting up an institutional debt restructuring mechanism to be established by an international treaty. This contractual approach to relations between borrower countries and their creditors consists of inserting new clauses into bonded loan agreements which would make it easier to negotiate rescheduling or restructuring during a financial crisis.

However, this solution is unsatisfactory because it can only be used on new loans and not on the entirety of the debt. Specifically, loan agreements would as a matter of course include a clause allowing a 'super majority' of private creditors (70–80 per cent) to sign a restructuring agreement that would apply to all creditors. Designed to thwart the rogue creditors who could block the entire process, this paltry proposal does nothing to resolve the problem of the lack of a fair and transparent regulation mechanism.

The United States maintains that a formal insolvency procedure would disadvantage emerging countries by influencing the flow of private capital into these countries or by significantly increasing its cost, since the procedure would put off private creditors from investing their money in these countries. However, there is no firm evidence of this potential risk. National bankruptcy legislation is not considered to be an impediment to domestic financing. On the contrary, nobody would expect to be able to provide loans at the national level without them being protected by a formal bankruptcy procedure. Moreover, the crux of the problem is not so much to do with the volume of investment as with its speculative nature.

The real objective of the United States' proposal is to nip the IMF's proposal in the bud.

The Washington compromise

In April 2002, in Washington, the G7 ministers of finance, with the IMF Development Committee, adopted a 'plan of action' designed to prevent financial crises, which is in fact nothing more than a compromise between the US plan and the IMF's proposal. The plan of action relegates the procedure proposed by the IMF to the role of 'the sword of Damocles' suspended above the heads of those private creditors who might be reluctant to accept the US plan. But in neither case is there any prospect of an international treaty, without which any prospect of establishing a formal procedure is ruined.

What alternatives?

In our analysis of the IMF proposal we have already set out a number of principles that we think should be incorporated into such a procedure. However, the analysis carried out by civil society and by independent experts, far from being based solely on the IMF proposal, already has a long history behind it. Some draw in part on the IMF proposals, while others develop radically different elements.

The principle they have in common is that while indebtedness (individual or collective) is a normal device for economic development, the lack of control or regulatory mechanism systematically leads to intolerable humanitarian disasters. It is therefore more necessary than ever to put into place measures to prevent over-indebtedness crises. But only a broad, fair and sustainable solution negotiated by all the interested parties will really be able to avert future insolvency crises. In many cases this kind of solution will mean rich countries and their private economic players relinquishing their loans.

In terms of the protection of international debtors, the basis of the thinking is, as often the case, the work on regulation developed at the national level. There are two main principles governing indebtedness problems at the national level: protecting debtors and holding them accountable. It is not a case of wronging either creditor or debtor, but of deciding fairly between the interests of both parties. For this to happen there will need to be independent legal adjudication drawing on legislative texts. The same principle forms the basis of thinking about the over-indebtedness of countries, such as, e.g., the appeal made by the UN secretary general for a 'debt arbitration system in order to weigh up the interests of sovereign creditors and debtors, and introduce better discipline in their relations'.

The idea of a state being declared bankrupt raises a lot of questions. This sort of procedure could in fact open the way to very worrying consequences (bankruptcy of public services, placing the finances of a state under trusteeship, etc.) that would only increase the domination of the IFIs and creditors over debtor states who are having difficulty with or have ceased repayments. For this reason, the bankruptcy procedures created for businesses cannot be applied to countries, but there are regulations at the national level adapted to sovereign debtors, in particular to local authorities. In such cases it is no longer a question of 'declaring bankruptcy', but of properly restructuring the debt, and cancelling part of it.

When it comes to establishing a fair and transparent mechanism for restructuring sovereign debt, the model that legal specialists have considered most frequently is the option of extending Article 9 of the American bankruptcy code (designed for sovereign debtors such as local authorities, as opposed to Article 11 which applies to businesses) to the international level. Article 9 established the rules of procedure for the bankruptcy of sovereign debtors in public law, such as local authorities. With a view to their unique situation, and more precisely in order for them to be able to maintain their public service role, the Article sets out the procedure for declaring sovereign debtors bankrupt, by placing limits on creditors' interference in the governmental sphere.

Protection of the debtor country's sovereignty

Article 9 protects the governmental powers in the name of the principle of sovereignty. The court cannot interfere in the governmental sphere: a court therefore cannot sequester a 'municipality' or dismiss elected representatives from their posts, unlike in the bankruptcy procedures that apply to businesses.

Protection of the debtors

A municipality cannot be made to stop providing certain public services that are essential for meeting the basic needs of their taxpayers (health, education, etc.) in order to honour its debts. Most democratic judicial systems recognize this principle of protecting the debtors' basic needs in the face of debt repayment obligations. In more general terms, the law recognizes that nobody can be forced to honour a contract that would seriously violate basic human rights.

At international level, the principle of debtor protection that exists at the national level is contained in the concept of 'justiciability' (i.e. the real implementation of fundamental economic and social rights). An international insolvency procedure would thus have to establish a ceiling for repayments, above which a state can no longer meet the basic human needs of its population (as defined in the Universal Declaration on Human Rights or the International Covenant on Economic, Cultural and Social Rights) and thus guarantee the sanctity of public spending on basic services. This ceiling should be the subject of independent and conflicting analysis and should progressively constitute jurisprudence for other debtor countries.

The right of all interested parties to be heard

Another characteristic of the Article, also on grounds of the unique position of sovereign debtors, is that it guarantees the right of citizens who will be affected by the solution to be heard and to oppose the proposed solution. With regard to the management of international debt, this principle implies (in contrast to the current process, both in the IFIs and the Paris Club) transparent and open negotiations with public hearings, as appropriate to their fair and democratic nature. Populations would thus be represented by civil society (NGOs, trade unions) or international organizations (UNICEF, ILO, WHO, etc.), who would defend their interests.

Furthermore, applying this principle would be a step towards debt relief procedures being appropriated by civil society, as is now advocated by the sponsors. In return, public debtors must suggest repayment conditions to the creditors that will allow them to recoup a reasonable proportion of their loans.

An independent arbitration authority

Overseeing these negotiations cannot be entrusted to either the creditors or the debtors, who both bear some responsibility for the over-indebtedness situation and have their own interests to protect; that role must be assumed by a neutral and independent institution. At present, however, there is no international judicial body capable of fulfilling this role.

Recourse to an ad hoc procedure is very common in the context of the arbitration procedure in international law, and is used particularly in bilateral procedures. This would be a fairer solution, in the sense that it would be able to better protect the interests of the debtors. This procedure anticipates the establishment of an arbitration committee in the form of an ad hoc panel comprising representatives of debtors and creditors in equal numbers. These representatives would then appoint a third party in order to allow the committee to make decisions by a simple majority.

However, a technical secretariat would be needed so as to guarantee the fairness of the process. It could be placed under the aegis of an institution that is neither creditor nor debtor, such as the United Nations or a specialized international arbitration institution. This secretariat would be responsible for supervising the evaluation process in accordance with international standards and ensuring its impartiality (by commissioning independent reports), for holding hearings and providing technical assistance to the arbitrators and to the organizations representing the various interested parties, in accordance with a procedure that still has to be defined. Above all, it would be responsible for ensuring the fairness of the procedure and the impartiality of the appointed third party.

However, the question arises of whether a process of this kind might really be capable of redressing the balance of power between debtors and creditors. A more formal and more restricting procedure might be needed. To this end, the establishment of a genuine permanent judicial body to arbitrate in negotiations between debtors and creditors on the basis of international law might be envisaged. Some legal specialists hold that the best solution would be to create a specialized chamber for this purpose within the International Court of Justice.

Establishing a procedure like this would require negotiation in a global political context. One possible route to this would be via an international conference on debt, under the auspices of the United Nations, which would work to review the 'sustainability' and legitimacy of debt.

The question of the illegitimacy of loans

In addition to defining repayment options and the need for the cancellation of loans, an arbitration court should also be able to rule on the legal and moral reprehensibility of some loans.

The category of illegitimate debts would include loans that did not serve the development of the population but were taken out by corrupt governments, with the collusion of the creditors. Loans acknowledged as illegitimate should be declared void. This question of the legitimacy of loans raises the problem of creditors' legal responsibility, based on the 'notion of the shared responsibility of the interested parties' which is inherent in traditional contract law.

Extending to the international level the concept of the banker's responsibility as defined in national law, which imposes on bankers an obligation of foresight with regard to the borrower's situation and the appropriateness of the credit, could thus provide a legal basis for delimiting responsibilities in building up an illegitimate debt. However, since the arbitration court would be a civil court, it would not be able to rule on the criminal responsibility of the perpetrators of these 'economic crimes'. It is therefore important to maintain in parallel the fight against international economic crime, by establishing and strengthening conventions and the appropriate international courts.

In this last context, the creditors could bear criminal responsibility in the case of having supported regimes responsible for war crimes or crimes against humanity. In this way, unscrupulous creditors could be convicted for collusion in misappropriation of funds, war crimes and crimes against humanity.

CONCLUSION

The various ideas for the establishment of a mechanism for restructuring sovereign debt are in part still on the drawing board. Unfortunately, time is short, because every day human lives are being sacrificed on a massive scale, in their thousands, even millions.

While we support the belated awakening of the international community, we reject the idea of declaring the countries of the South bankrupt, which would equate to the bankruptcy of development and to placing countries with an extremely reduced margin of manoeuvrability under tutelage. On the contrary, we should be motivated to seek a broad, fair and sustainable solution to the debt problem with the objective of sustainable development.

Once again, we warn against the temptation of power and undivided control of the rich countries, because there is a tremendous risk of creating a 'creditor super-club' which would, by combining the strength of the financial markets and the domination of the IFIs, cause the populations of developing countries, who suffer daily as a result of underdevelopment, to bear once again too heavy a burden.

We also warn against the temptation to only concern oneself with countries in the event of a major crisis. All too often it is by then already too late and the country is already overwhelmed, as has been shown by Argentina. The priority should therefore be preventing crises, by controlling speculative financial flows and through the possibility of having recourse to a debt restructuring mechanism, including debt cancellation, as soon as the alarm bells start to ring for over-indebted countries.

Finally, it is clear that re-establishing the process of sustainable development for the countries of the South will require efforts on the part of the countries of the North and their economic actors. These readjustments to the world economy, currently left to its own devices, will not be without cost, in the area of the environment, debt or international commerce. But today this is almost entirely supported by developing countries and their populations. This cost will need to be shared more fairly in order to build a common future.

13

The Illegitimacy of Debt

Lidy Nacpil (Jubilee South)

THE JUBILEE SOUTH PERSPECTIVE ON DEBT

The debt problem must be understood in its historical, political and economic context. Such an understanding points to the illegitimacy of debt.

The indebtedness of the South is the result of the exploitation and control of the resources, economies and peoples of the South throughout the history of colonization, neocolonization and capitalist globalization. The resulting underdevelopment, poverty, lack of financial resources and reliance on imports created the 'need' for external capital infusion in the form of aid, investments and loans. Northern creditors use debt as an instrument for the continued plunder of the South, actively cultivating the need to borrow and relentlessly pushing loans to governments and private corporations in the South. These creditors are banks, corporations, northern governments, and international financial institutions (IFIs).

In addition to making huge profits through lending, northern creditors used debt and credit as leverage for economic conditionalities on the South, with the acquiescence, if not active collaboration, of local elites. These economic conditionalities perpetuate the relations of dominance and exploitation and the concentration of wealth and power in the global capitalist system, and consequently lead to greater impoverishment in the South. Aside from the creditors, local elites were the beneficiaries of these loans, and not the peoples of the South. Many of these debts lined the pockets of corrupt government officials. There were also huge debts of private corporations that were guaranteed by governments and subsequently assumed and transformed into public debts, paid for with public funds.

Many debts were contracted through illegitimate means (with the use of bribery or fraud, circumventing or violating established procedures), and/or contracted by illegitimate parties (dictatorships, apartheid governments etc.), and/or with illegitimate terms (e.g. floating rates which led to very high interest rates), and/or for illegitimate purposes (projects and policies harmful to people, communities and the environment).

The servicing of these huge debts has placed an unbearable burden on countries in the South, and has a terrible impact on our people, economies and environment. In many countries in the South, payment on interest alone is the single biggest item in public spending. Such debt has actually been paid many times over by the people, in financial, economic, social and environmental terms.

For all these reasons, Jubilee South regards the so-called debt of the South as illegitimate and not owed by the people of the South. Therefore, the people of the South should not be made to pay this debt. It is a grave injustice that the people of the South are made to pay these debts in the face of urgent needs for survival.

Even more fundamentally unjust is that these debts are not owed by the people of the South and have in fact been used against them in many ways. Rather, the peoples and countries of the South are in fact creditors of an enormous historical, social and ecological debt of the North. It is the North that owes the South.

OUR STRUGGLE: ENDING DEBT DOMINATION

More than simply debt relief, Jubilee South is committed to the struggle to end debt domination and build an alternative order. Jubilee South has united on a set of general calls and demands that articulate the Jubilee South framework and serve as strategic goals and direction for its work:

- Collective repudiation by southern governments of all illegitimate debts. We dare to call for debt repudiation. The issue of illegitimacy makes debt repudiation not only an imperative for survival and development, but also the repudiation of illegitimate debts should be upheld as the right of peoples and nations and an obligation of the governments of the South.
- Total debt cancellation without conditionalities by creditors. The issue of the illegitimacy of debts clearly shows that debt cancellation is not a matter of charity towards the poor countries of the South; it is not about whether southern countries can or cannot afford to pay their debts. Debt cancellation is an urgent issue of survival, but it is also fundamentally a matter of justice, and it is justice for all countries of the South.
- Rechanneling of public funds away from debt service to ensure that they are used primarily for people's welfare: basic services and equitable and sustainable development.
- Putting an end to neoliberal economic conditionalities and policies.
- Full restitution and reparations by northern creditors for the human, social and environmental damage caused by their debt policies, structural adjustment programmes and other economic policies, and their exploitation of the peoples and resources of the South.
- The recognition of southern peoples and countries as legitimate creditors of a historical, social and ecological debt owed by the North.
- Systemic, structural and policy changes that will get the countries of the South out of the debt trap, prevent the repetition of these problems and promote political and economic democracy and equity, popular empowerment and sustainable development.
- Transformation of the global capitalist economic system, building a new world economic order that is people-centred, equitable, gender-fair, sustainable and democratic.

Our basic strategy

1. Developing and strengthening our movements in the South, waging local and national struggles.
2. Globalizing our resistance and struggles on the basis of the strength of our local and national movements.
3. Forging South-North solidarity based on a common agenda and vision.

Our programme

We recognize that our work entails a comprehensive programme that involves the following:

- Promoting a critical and liberating framework on debt among our people.
- Challenging and changing the dominant discourse on the debt problem, towards a discourse based on the framework of illegitimacy of debt and the assertion that the peoples of the South are in fact the creditors of historical, social, economic and ecological debt.
- Building and strengthening the constituency, political base and organizational means that will give force and flesh to the global, collective southern movement against debt and capitalist globalization.
- Developing global and regional campaigns, and strengthening local and national campaigns and struggles on debt, for immediate as well as longer-term strategic goals.

Campaigning on the illegitimacy on debt means:

- Waging specific campaigns that serve our strategic goals.
- Translating our framework and strategic calls into campaign plans and calls that are appropriate to the particular political and economic situations we face in our different countries, appropriate to specific conjunctures in regional and global arenas.
- Aiming for immediate and medium-term objectives and calls (congruent with our strategic goals) that engage and challenge creditors, rally our people to action, represent political advances in our struggles and concrete victories, including changes in processes and policies that will broaden the discourse, increase democratic empowerment and participation, and provide specific improvements in the conditions of our people.

Specific Campaigns

Jubilee South continues its campaigning efforts on the illegitimacy of debt through specific campaigns conducted at global and regional levels, and through support for national campaigns.

Each specific campaign will contribute towards asserting and popularizing the JS framework of illegitimacy of debt, mobilize popular action around particular issues of illegitimacy of debt, and put forward specific calls and demands about these issues. Campaigning includes the following components:

- Research and policy studies
- Constituency building; education for a campaign constituency
- Alliance work and networking
- Public information and influencing public opinion
- Media work
- Engaging in policy debates
- Lobbying and public pressure
- Political actions and mobilizations

14

A CALL TO ACTION

The debt crisis remains unresolved. Wealth continues to be transferred from the South to the North through debt payments. Financial transfers remain negative because of falling investments and declining terms of trade in the South. New loans are made to rollover old debts in a vicious cycle of indebtedness. All this continues to result in unmitigated human suffering, especially for women and children, and ecological degradation in poor countries, as the crises in Argentina and other nations remind us. The current situation is unsustainable and immoral.

At its core, the debt problem is one of profoundly unequal power relations. The imbalance of power in the global system of governance has become even more skewed. We live in an age of empire, where one superpower can unilaterally decide to invade a country on an unfounded premise, where one superpower can flout international law with impunity, and where one superpower can quash even a weak response to the debt problem, such the Sovereign Debt Restructuring Mechanism.

The debt crisis cannot be de-linked from economic globalization and the whole unjust economic system. We are thus facing a neoliberal framework and strategy articulated through the International Monetary Fund, World Bank and World Trade Organization – institutions that serve the economic interests of the powerful at the expense of many people's human rights and environmental integrity.

Moreover, in many of our own countries, we find governments that are subservient to the neoliberal policy dictates of these international financial and economic institutions and the interests behind them. All initiatives, including the Heavily Indebted Poor Country initiative and the Poverty Reduction Strategy Paper approach, have never addressed the roots of the problem and have even failed in their own terms.

Yet there are reasons for optimism and hope. We live in exciting times: an expanding global civil society has been coming together in an unprecedented way, in the World Social Forum process and elsewhere, and mobilizing around fundamental concerns of justice and human dignity that touch us all. Debt is one such issue where justice is at the heart of the matter.

There is a widening of the discussion on debt to include ecological concerns and the historical legacy of colonialism and neocolonialism. The issue of unjust trade has become more prominent within civil society debates. It is clear that debt and trade are inextricably linked in terms of permanent structural adjustment and declining terms of trade and balance of payments.

Now, more than ever, there is a need to develop, mobilize and strengthen social movements within and between countries. We have to forge common understandings and unity, both within the debt movement and between debt, trade, environmental movements and the global justice movement as a whole, so that all can work together for the cancellation of illegitimate debts and the building of a more just, life-affirming global economic system. Together, engaged civil society comprises that 'other power' or counter-power to global hegemony.

The following strategies and specific actions will help us move forward on the debt problem:

- Conduct debt audits to advance the issue of illegitimate debt and ecological debt (countries such as Brazil, Ecuador and the Democratic Republic of Congo can be used as case studies).
- Consider the possibility of a World Commission on Foreign Debt and Audit.
- Demand the cancellation of Iraq's odious debt and demand reparations for the Iraqi people through their legitimately constituted government.
- Continue to develop and explore international laws and legal mechanisms to address illegitimate debt and ecological debt, including undertaking a collective analysis and publication of case studies on illegitimate and odious debts and looking at the possibility of bringing a case to the International Court of Justice.
- Involve parliamentarians in the discussion of illegitimate debt, ecological debt and a fair and transparent arbitration process.
- Confront the Paris Club and other creditor clubs.
- Continue to mobilize at international meetings and other events such as the WTO Ministerial in Cancun, the annual meetings of the IFIs, the United Nations General Assembly, and the African heads of state meetings.
- Link the issues of debt and trade more deliberately through studies and active participation of debt movements in Cancun and trade-related events.
- Reappropriate and maximize the UN Economic and Social Council as a forum for discussing illegitimate debt, ecological debt and a fair and transparent arbitration process, plus other alternative initiatives for socio-economic transformation.
- Bring the concept of ecological debt to environmental meetings and fora.
- Identify and publicize 'reckless lenders' to discredit the creditors.
- Call for an international week of action on debt, coinciding with International Human Rights Day.
- Support the Southern People's Ecological Debt Alliance.
- Conduct research on the impacts of debt servicing, debt and women, debt and privatization, debt and PRSPs, and debt and militarism.
- Hold various conferences and meetings on debt and such subjects as a public referendum on non-payment of debt at national and global levels, ecological debt, restitution and reparations.

15

Summary of Proceedings

From 30 June to 2 July 2003, 30 debt activists from various campaigns and movements devoted to eradicating the external debt problem of poor countries came together at the Ecumenical Centre in Geneva, Switzerland, from all over the world to participate in a workshop organized by the World Council of Churches on Illegitimate Debt and Arbitration. The workshop set itself three challenging objectives:

- Assess the ongoing debt campaigns in view of current geopolitics in the world;
- Explore the relationship between the Illegitimacy of Debt, Ecological Debt and Fair and Transparent Arbitration Process; and
- Identify urgent issues for focusing our work, strategies and concrete actions for revitalizing the debt movement.

The debt movement is rich and wealthy in its approaches to resolving the debt problem. In recognition of this richness, we present our discussion in the form of a summary.

The debt crisis remains unresolved. Wealth continues to be transferred from the South to the North through debt payments, among others. Financial transfers remain negative because of falling investments and declining terms of trade in the South. New loans are made to roll-over old debts in a vicious cycle of indebtedness. All this continues to result in unmitigated human suffering, especially of women and children, and ecological degradation in poor countries, as the crises in Argentina and other countries remind us. The current situation is unsustainable and immoral.

At core, the debt problem is one of profoundly unequal power relations. The balance of power in the global governance system has become even more skewed. We live in an age of empire where one superpower can unilaterally decide to invade a country on an unfounded premise, where that one superpower can flout international law with impunity, and where that one superpower can quash even a weak response to the debt problem such as the Sovereign Debt Restructuring Mechanism.

The debt crisis cannot be de-linked from economic globalization and the whole unjust economic system. We are thus facing a neoliberal framework and strategy articulated through the International Monetary Fund, World Bank and World Trade Organization (WTO) – institutions that serve the economic interests of the powerful at the expense of many people's human rights and environmental integrity.

Moreover, in many of our own countries, we find governments that are subservient to the neoliberal policy dictates of these international financial and economic institutions and the interests behind them. All initiatives that have emanated from these institutions, including the Heavily Indebted Poor Country initiative and the Poverty Reduction Strategy Paper approach, have never sought to address the roots of the problem and have even failed in their own terms.

Yet there are reasons for optimism and hope. We live in exciting times: an expanding global civil society has been coming together in an unprecedented way, in the World Social Forum process and elsewhere, and mobilizing around fundamental concerns of justice and human dignity that touch us all. The debt issue is one such issue where justice is at the heart of the matter.

There is a growing echo on the debt issue and widening of the discussion to include ecological concerns and the historical legacy of colonialism and neocolonialism. The issue of unjust trade has become more prominent within civil society debate. Nonetheless, it is clear that debt and trade are inextricably linked in terms both of permanent structural adjustment and of declining terms of trade and the balance of payments.

Now, more than ever, there is a need to further develop, mobilize and strengthen social movements within and between countries. We have to forge common understanding and unity within the debt movement and between debt, trade, environmental movements and the global justice movement as a whole so that we may all work together for the cancellation of Illegitimate Debts and the building of a more just, life-affirming global economic system. Together, engaged civil society comprises that "other power" or counter power.

We explored the Illegitimacy of Debt, Ecological debt and Fair and Transparent Arbitration Process approaches as well as the relationships and linkages between these approaches.

Justice is a common thread that runs though all three approaches to resolve the debt problem.

In the Illegitimacy of Debt approach, illegitimate debts include those debts that were taken under illegitimate means (fraud and corruption) and illegitimate terms (floating interest rates), by illegitimate parties (dictatorial governments), and for illegitimate purposes (projects that did not benefit peoples and in fact worked against them such as those that financed wars and harmed the environment). In principle, such debts should be cancelled and/or repudiated. Discussions took place on the circumstances under which countries could repudiate debt, how to avoid retaliation by creditors, and how unilateral repudiation could undermine the entire financial system and create a crisis in the system with far-reaching effects.

The Ecological Debt provides an empowering and liberating framework for peoples in the South in helping to change mindsets from Southern countries/peoples as debtors to Southern countries/peoples as creditors and in recognizing environmental concerns and the plunder of Southern resources by the North since colonial times. It is an important element of the Illegitimacy of Debt approach. We discussed how to apply restitution and reparation. We realised that more study and research on the concept of Ecological Debt in the North may be needed.

Arbitration processes that are free and transparent are a possible mechanism to deal with unsustainable Illegitimate Debt and Ecological Debt. It seeks to help to redress the unfair power balance between debtors and creditors in resolving debt and could serve as a protective buffer for countries repudiating debt. We discussed the danger of how the arbitration process could reflect the current unequal distribution of power and enforce the status quo. Other questions arose: What laws and rules can be used as basis for arbitration? Is such a mechanism feasible in the present international circumstances? Who can fill the role of an independent third party that will reach a decision? Is it appropriate to put creditors at the same table as sovereign states?

We found that there is a need to push for the conduct of audits of debts at the national and global, and citizen and government levels.

In moving forward in addressing the debt problem, we identified the following strategies and concrete actions:

- Conduct processes of debt auditing to advance the issue of Illegitimate Debt and Ecological Debt (countries such as Brazil, Ecuador and the Democratic Republic of Congo can be used as case studies);
- Consider the possibility of a World Commission on Foreign Debt and Audit;
- Demand the cancellation of Iraq's odious debt and demand reparations for the Iraqi people through their legitimately-constituted government;
- Continue to develop and explore international laws and legal mechanisms to address Illegitimate Debt and Ecological Debt including undertaking a collective study and publication of case studies on illegitimate and odious debts and looking at the possibility of bringing a case to the International Court of Justice;
- Involve parliamentarians in the discussion on Illegitimate Debt, Ecological Debt and Fair and Transparent Arbitration Process;
- Confront the Paris Club and other creditor clubs;
- Continue to mobilize at international meetings and other events such as the WTO Ministerial in Cancun, the annual meetings of the international financial institutions, the United Nations (UN) General Assembly, and the African Heads of State meetings;
- Link the issues of debt and trade more deliberately through studies and active participation of debt movements in Cancun and trade-related events;
- Re-appropriate and maximize the UN Economic and Social Council as a forum for discussing Illegitimate Debt, Ecological Debt and Fair and Transparent Arbitration Process and other alternative initiatives for socio-economic transformation;
- Take concept of ecological debt in environmental meetings and fora;
- Identify and publicize "reckless lenders" to discredit the creditors;
- Call for an international week of actions on debt coinciding with International Human Rights Day;
- Support the Southern People's Ecological Debt Alliance;
- Conduct research on impacts of debt servicing, debt and women, debt and privatization, debt and PRSPs, and debt and militarism, among others; and
- Hold various conferences and meetings on debt including the following: Conference on How to Work Out Payment, Public Referendum on Non-

Payment of Debt at national and global levels, Conference on Ecological Debt, Restitution and Reparations, South-South Summit in India before the World Social Forum, Summit on Odious Debt in 2004, Meeting on Ecological Debt in October 2003, International Conference on Debt in Africa in 2004, International Meeting on Fair and Transparent Arbitration Process in Guayaquil, Ecuador in 2004, third International Seminar on Odious Debt and International Law in Amsterdam in December 2004, Africa Jubilee South Meeting in Mali in December 2003, and Parliamentarian's Forum on Illegitimate Debt.

Appendix

LIST OF PARTICIPANTS

Ms Sofia Walan, Christian Council of Sweden

Mr. Tomas Tozicka, Jubilee Czech

Ms Susanne Luithlen, Erlassjahr.de, Jubilee Germany

Mr. Fredrik Gjernes, Norwegian Church Aid

Mr. Peter Lanzet, Evangelischer Entwicklungsdienst e.V./EED

Ms Barbara Kalima, AFRODAD

Mr. Alejandro Bendaña, Center for International Studies, Managua

Mr. Jean Merckaert, Comité Catholique contre la Faim et pour le Développement - CCFD

Mr. Eric Toussaint, Comité pour l'Annulation de la Dette du Tiers Monde (CATDM)

Mr. John Dillon, Kairos, Canadian Ecumenical Justice Initiatives

Mr. William Hugo Arias Palacios, General Coordinator, Jubilee 2000 Red Guyaquil

Ms Maria Dyveke Styve, SLUG, Norwegian Campaign for Cancellation of Third World Debt

Ms Aurora Donoso, Acción Ecologica, Quito

Mr. Malcolm Damon, Director, Economic Justice Network of Fellowship of Christian Councils in Southern Africa (FOCCISA)

Ms Liza Gay C. Maglinao, Jubilee South Movement, Quezon City

Ms Sandra Maria Quintela Lopes, PACS / Campanha Jubieu Sul Brasil

Ms Shelly Emalin Rao, Ecumenical Center for Research, Education & Advocacy (ECREA), Suva

Mr. Kusfiardi, Koalisi Anti-Utang, Anti Debt Coalition, Jakarta

Mr. Brian Ashley, Alternative Information and Development Centre (AIDC)

Ms Georgine Kenge Djeutane, Jubilee 2000 Cameroun Ecumenical Service for Peace

Mr. Alain Saumon, Comité pour l'Annulation de la Dette du Tiers Monde - CADTM France

Mr. MP Giyose, Jubilee South Africa

Rev. David Ugolor, African Network for Environmental and Economic Justice (ANEEJ)

Mr. Nicolas Maystre, CADTM Suisse

Mr. Hugo Ruiz Diaz, CADTM - Belgias

Mr. Martin Junge, Lutheran World Federation

Ms Linda Hartke, Ecumenical Advocacy Alliance

Mr. Peter Prove, Human Rights, Lutheran World Federation

Mr. Marcos Sanchez, Spanish Interpreter

Ms Silvia Lee-Rieben, Spanish Interpreter

Mr. Rogate R. Mshana, Economic Justice, Programme Executive, World Council of Churches

Ms Athena Peralta, Women and Economic Consultant, World Council of Churches

L'impression et le façonnage ont été réalisés
à l'Imprimerie LUSSAUD - 85200 Fontenay-le-Comte

Dépôt légal 2e trimestre 2004 - n° 3739 – N° d'impression : 203522